How to Buy Your Perfect

Wedding Dress

Ronald Rothstein

and

Mara Urshel

with Todd Lyon

Illustrations by Monica Rangne

A Lark Production
A Fireside Book
Published by Simon & Schuster
New York London Toronto Sydney Singapore

FIRESIDE
Rockefeller Center
1230 Avenue of the Americas
New York, NY 10020

For information regarding special discounts for bulk purchases,
please contact Simon & Schuster Special Sales at 1-800-456-6798
or business@simonandschuster.com

Designed by Diane Hobbing of Snap-Haus Graphics

Manufactured in the United States of America
10 9 8 7 6 5 4 3 2 1
Library of Congress Cataloging-in-Publication data is available
ISBN 0-7432-2581-3

CONTENTS

INTRODUCTION

Congratulations! You're getting married. Your wedding day promises to be the most exciting and memorable day of your life. It may take a year or more of dedicated planning, but at the end of that long road will be a perfect moment when you take a glorious walk that leads to your future. There will be flowers and music, family and friends; there will be tuxedos, cameras, limousines, and flower girls. In that swirl of champagne and hankies, at the center of all that magic, there will be you. Your face will glow, your eyes will shine, and you will be resplendent in the most beautiful gown in the world.

But let's back up a minute, shall we? Between today and the day of your dreams, there is an enormous amount of work to do. You've got to find a location, order invitations, hire a caterer, audition bands, apply for a marriage license . . . and that's just for starters. Among the 3,452 decisions you'll have to make between now and then is one that looms large: What will you wear? This question can't be taken lightly. After all, it is the dress—much more than the flowers, the table linens, the place cards, or even the vows—that ultimately defines you as a bride.

In the grand scheme of wedding planning, shopping for your wedding dress comes before booking a photographer and registering for gifts—about nine to twelve months before the big day. Though most wedding dresses are custom-made, their cost is relatively small—in fact, it's likely you'll spend only 6 to 15 percent of your entire wedding budget on your gown, headpiece, veil, shoes, accessories, undergarments, hair, and makeup. And compared to, say, the cost of the reception, that's a bargain. But whether you spend under $500 or more than $20,000 on your attire, your wedding gown will probably be the most expensive garment you'll ever buy, as well as the most unforgettable.

Brides come in all sizes, ages, and sets of circumstances. Have you been clipping pictures of wedding gowns out of magazines since you were six? Or have you sworn for forty years that you'd never get married, only to get caught in Cupid's crossfire? You might be twenty years old and blissfully betrothed to your first love or fifty years old and following your heart down the aisle for the third time. Are you planning a simple ceremony on the beach or hosting three hundred guests at a sit-down dinner? No matter what your status, the dress of your dreams is out there.

Finding it might not be easy, however. Shopping for a wedding gown is not like picking out a winter coat or a spring suit. The stores are different, the merchandise is different, and the process is nothing like anything you've ever experienced. You're going to need advice and guidance to help you chart a course between what's in your head to what you'll be wearing when you walk down the aisle. And no one can navigate that course better than the experts at Kleinfeld.

Introduction

A SHORT HISTORY OF KLEINFELD

Kleinfeld is the legendary couture bridal salon founded in 1941 in the Bay Ridge section of Brooklyn, New York. When Isadore Kleinfeld first opened its doors, furs were the main attraction, but it wasn't long before the shop's fashionable wedding gowns took center stage. By 1968 the Kleinfeld company, under the direction of Isadore's daughter Hedda and her husband, Jack, was specializing in bridal wear and had become a mecca for brides-to-be, who counted on Kleinfeld to bring them the largest selection of gowns in the world.

We had the privilege of seeing Hedda and Jack Schachter in action. This was back in the 1980s, when one of us (Mara) had the position of senior vice president of Saks Fifth Avenue. Hedda and Jack were thinking about selling Kleinfeld, and we had been coaxed by a potential buyer to "take a look" at the famous salon in Brooklyn. We went, and there they were, running around, still 500 percent involved with their brides. Hedda wore black Reebok sneakers, a tartan skirt, and a tape measure around her neck. She was a brilliant woman, truly the fashion maven of bridal. She was the first American bridal store owner to go to Europe and hand-pick designer gowns and evening dresses; they caused a sensation. Hedda told us that running Kleinfeld was "like hosting a huge party every day."

We passed on the opportunity to get involved with Kleinfeld but not for long. Some years later, after we had established our own consulting company, we were contacted by the Boston-based corporation that had bought Kleinfeld. They were looking for a high-end retail executive to help guide the salon into the twenty-first century. In July 1999, we joined with our principal partners—Hollywood actor/mogul Wayne Rogers, entrepreneur and former Duke University business professor W. Clay Hamner, and our friend and attorney Marvin Goldstein—and a handful of close friends and favorite relatives and bought Kleinfeld outright. One of our first tasks was to give the space a major makeover.

Today, Kleinfeld looks from the outside like a small, exclusive boutique with artistic window displays. Inside, the thirty-thousand-square-foot Kleinfeld is not just a salon but an emporium. Close to one thousand designer dresses—including fairy-tale ball gowns, contemporary sheaths, and an exclusive European couture collection—are displayed in elegant showrooms. Behind the doors at the corner of Fifth Avenue and 82nd Street in Brooklyn, clients are lavished with the kind of personal attention usually reserved for queens and celebrities. At the salon, the bride is invited into her own fitting room, from which she emerges now and then to admire herself in Kleinfeld's multimirrored "twirling area." Meanwhile, behind the scenes, some 75 fitters, seamstresses, embroiderers, beaders, and pressers work to make wedding day dreams come true.

At the heart of the Kleinfeld experience is the relationship between the client and her personal bridal consultant. From the minute she walks through the door until the day she walks down the aisle, the future bride is guided by an expert who is part stylist, part counselor, and part fairy godmother. The consultant learns all she can about the bride, her wedding plans, and her personal style. Armed with information, the consultant presents the bride with a selection of dresses that suits her requirements and restrictions, including her body type, her wedding style, and her budget.

When the future bride finds the one dress that melts her heart, it's time for Kleinfeld's artisans to go to work. Fittings, alterations, and more fittings are assigned to a fitter who watches over every phase of the gown's creation and ensures that everything—from the drape of the skirt to the beading on the bodice—is perfect.

We've thrown our hearts and souls into making Kleinfeld the best bridal salon in the world. For us, it is not just a business, it is a labor of love. And every day, we are rewarded with joy. Nothing is more satisfying to us than seeing a bride-to-be standing before a mirror, glowing with happiness, gorgeous in a gown that's more beautiful than she'd ever dared wish for.

Every bride is precious to us, and we take her hopes and dreams personally. In fact, we get so involved with our brides and their families that we're invited to hundreds of weddings every year—and attend as many as humanly possible.

Though we might not make it to your wedding, and you may not be able to visit us in Brooklyn, we've done the next best thing. After decades of offering priceless advice and consultations to brides one-on-one, Kleinfeld has come to you.

Introduction

How to Buy Your Perfect Wedding Dress condenses sixty years of wedding dress wisdom into one comprehensive guide. With it, you can save time and stress by reviewing all your options before you ever set foot in a salon. Take a close look at gown styles. See which ones make you swoon and which ones leave you cold. Learn about headpieces, veils, and trains; become an armchair expert on beading, lace, fabric, and trim. Get to know your body type from a wedding gown's point of view and gain the tools to help you flatter your figure. You can pick up pointers on when to shop, how to shop, what to bring, whom to bring, what to expect from the fitting process, how to make your gown last forever—and, especially, how to make your shopping experience fun, relaxed, and smashingly successful.

At the end of it all, you will be an informed bride. Better yet, you will be a Kleinfeld bride. Which, as any insider will tell you, is a very special bride to be.

Introduction

Chapter One

Define Your Wedding Style

Today's wedding gown marketplace offers a delightful confusion of options and styles. The future bride is faced with selections that veer wildly from sleek, form-fitting gowns to Cinderella confections. She can choose to look like a medieval queen or a fairy princess; she can don a tailored suit or bare her midriff and expose a diamond-studded belly.

With so many choices leaping out from the pages of magazines, online bridal sites, and the windows of alluring shops, it's smart to start your wedding gown odyssey with a simple process of elimination. Question #1: What style of wedding do you want? Formal? Informal? Or somewhere in between?

Look at the following definitions and see which one best matches your vision. If you can adopt one of these categories as your own, it will help you define your general bridal style and inform all kinds of future decisions, from flower arrangements to guest accommodations.

THE FORMAL WEDDING

Formal comes in many packages; many of them are lavish, pricey, and elaborate. For Melissa Rivers's formal wedding, Manhattan's Plaza Hotel was transformed into a scene from eighteenth-century imperialist Russia complete with white birch trees, antique candelabra, and footmen in powdered wigs. At Kleinfeld, we outfitted a bride who rode to her 1,200-guest reception in a glass carriage pulled by six white horses. Upon her arrival, she and her groom were heralded by trumpeters in elaborate uniforms. But whether it takes place in a palace or in the church around the corner, virtually all formal weddings have a few things in common.

A formal wedding is one in which you will most likely:

- Have a religious ceremony in a cathedral, church, synagogue, or other place of worship.
- Have a full reception in a hotel ballroom, a mansion, museum, country club, cruise ship, or other upscale location.
- Have assigned dinner seating at the reception.
- Outfit your groom and his groomsmen in tuxedos, traditional morning coats, or other formal attire.
- Dress your attendants in matching gowns and shoes.

For a formal wedding, you'll probably want to limit your gown choices to those that are:

- White or ivory.
- Floor length.

- Outfitted with a long veil and perhaps a train.
- Made from luxurious fabrics.
- Possibly graced by long sleeves or accessorized with gloves.
- Detailed with pearls, lace, jewels, beading, sequins, and crystals.
- Topped with a tiara or other regal headpiece.

THE SEMIFORMAL WEDDING

This vast category includes all sorts of weddings, some of which might mix formal with informal. Actress Kate Winslet of *Titanic* fame, for instance, was married in her family church but held her reception at a local pub, where guests ate "bangers and mash" (sausages and whipped potatoes) and danced the jig. More often, however, a semiformal wedding is one in which you might choose to:

- Have your ceremony in a chapel, a garden, a private home, or a sentimental or scenic location.
- Host a sit-down or buffet-style catered reception outdoors under a tent or welcome your guests at a hall, restaurant, seaside pavilion, private function room, or similar location.
- Dress your groom in a tux, a dinner jacket, or a suit and tie.
- Have only a few attendants and groomsmen in coordinated outfits.
- Skip certain traditions, such as the receiving line or announced introductions.

Define Your Wedding Style

For a semiformal wedding, your gown choices might include:

- White, silk white, ivory, or pale pastel tones.
- Ankle-length, tea-length (just above the ankle), or intermission hemline (anywhere between the knee and the ankle).
- Styles ranging from historic costume to avant-garde.
- A modest train or no train.
- A subtle headpiece with or without a veil.

THE INFORMAL WEDDING

Often, an outdoor setting is the star at an informal wedding. However, like its formal and semiformal sisters, the informal affair can take many forms. Consider the nuptials of actor Russell Means, who is of Sioux heritage. At his wedding to Pearl Daniel, who is half Navajo, traditional Native American singers and dancers performed to the sound of drumbeats, and guests dined on buffalo and mutton. The bride wore an eggplant-colored blouse, a velveteen skirt, and moccasins.

Equally informal but entirely different in spirit was the wedding of a Kleinfeld bride who bought a white velvet sheath decorated with pearls. The dress could have passed for an evening gown, and that was the point: she and her fiancé, a pianist, invited all their friends to a New Year's Eve party at their home. Close to midnight, the couple announced that they were getting married right there and then. After the ceremony, their surprised and delighted guests were treated to a private concert performed by the newly minted groom.

An informal wedding might include:

- Nontraditional or self-written vows taken in a private home, on a pier, on the beach, on a rooftop, or in a nightclub.
- A buffet-style dinner or picnic, clambake, barbecue, or similar affair with nonassigned seating.
- Groom outfitted in expressive, unconventional, or low-key attire.
- Few or no attendants.
- Creative new traditions in place of the garter ritual, bouquet tossing, cake cutting, and so on.

An informal bride might consider wearing:

- A dress that strays from traditional shades of white into colors such as lavender, pale yellow, blush pink, and so forth.
- A two-piece dress, a suit, a tunic, a sundress, a sarong, a simple sheath, or pants.
- A crown of fresh flowers.
- Hair jewelry in lieu of a headpiece.
- Dress details that reflect or celebrate the setting, such as leaf or shell motifs.

TIME OF YEAR

Another important (and undeniably practical) consideration when shopping for a gown is the season in which you plan to marry. Years ago, a bride simply wouldn't wear a strapless gown in January; today, those notions of seasonally correct attire have been thrown out. However, there are fabric and style choices that lend themselves nicely to each season.

In the spring, when heavy winter garb has been abandoned but the weather is still unpredictable, you might try:

- Fibers and fabrics such as silk, satin, tulle, organza, and charmeuse.
- A hat or a decorated headband, with or without a veil.
- Tea-length or intermission hemline dress.
- Cap sleeves or off-the-shoulder neckline with short gloves.
- Open-toed shoes or slingbacks.

Summer weddings can be balmy, breezy, or blistering. Smart options include:

- Cool fibers and fabrics like satin, linen, chiffon, tulle, organza, or gazar.
- Spaghetti-strap, halter, strapless, or backless styles.
- Two-piece dresses with hints of bare skin at the midriff.
- Short, medium-length, or ankle-length skirts.
- Wide-brimmed, polished straw hats or picture hats.
- Fresh flower headpieces, with or without a veil.
- Dressy sandals.

For autumn weddings, when the frost is on the pumpkin and the parties have moved inside, good choices might include:

- Medium-weight fibers and fabrics such as taffeta, raw silk, shantung silk, silk satin, and silk gazar.
- Sweetheart, bateaux, or scoop necklines.
- A shawl.
- Three-quarter-length sleeves or above-the-elbow gloves.
- A mantilla made of heavy lace.
- A lightweight cape or capelet.

Winter weddings are romantic but risky weatherwise. Though a good cover-up can keep you warm all day and night, you might consider:

- Fabrics such as satin, brocade, velvet, and mikado.
- Long sleeves.
- Higher necklines.
- Headpieces that incorporate a hat (possibly made from fur or feathers).
- Fur or faux fur trim, stole, or muff.
- Kid leather gloves.
- Wedding boots.
- A bridal coat or cape.

DAY OR EVENING?

Your next thought should be the time of day: morning, afternoon, or evening. Again, old etiquette books made a strong distinction among appropriate styles for weddings that took place in broad daylight and those that happened at night. Though such boundaries have faded considerably over the years, it's still true that evening weddings tend to be a bit fancier than daytime weddings. Heavy beading and sequins are friends of the night, while more diaphanous materials— tulle, organza, taffeta—flutter beautifully in the light of day.

PRICE CONSIDERATIONS

Your wedding gown might be the most expensive article of clothing you purchase in your whole life. Or not. Sharp-eyed, budget-minded brides might be able to pick up a dress on sale, right off the rack, for as little as $300, then pay additional alteration fees out of pocket. The sentimental bride might honor her heritage— and save a bundle—by wearing her mother's or her grandmother's wedding gown (again, alteration fees will apply). But the average bride can expect to pay a minimum of $800 for her gown, depending on her taste and where she shops. Designer gowns usually start at about $1,700 and can cost upward of $10,000.

A general rule is that the bride's attire should represent 6 to 15 percent of the entire wedding budget. That final figure should include the cost of a headpiece and veil (about $150–$700), bridal shoes ($60–$300), undergarments (figure $50–$120), and accessories such as jewelry, purse, gloves, wrap, and so forth (allow $100–$500 or more, depending on the look you're going for).

If you're ordering a custom gown, as most brides do, you can expect to pay a 50 or 60 percent deposit to the bridal salon. It's smart to pay this deposit with a credit card, because it offers more protection to you in case there's a problem with the dress or a breach-of-contract situation.

DEFINING YOUR PERSONAL STYLE

Back when the fabulous Jackie O. was Miss Jacqueline Bouvier, she wore a highly decorated gown to her wedding to John F. Kennedy. Jackie thought the dress looked like a lamp-shade and later confessed to a friend: "It was the dress my mother wanted me to wear, and I hated it."

How can you avoid the Jackie trap? By narrowing down your choices to those that reflect your truest self. If you wear tailored clothes in your day-to-day life, and have a closet full of minimalist suits and conservative shoes, chances are you won't be comfortable in a fanciful gown with miles of taffeta skirting—even if you (or your mother) develop a crush on it while you're in the bridal salon. Conversely, if you're a girl who loves extravagant garb and lives to dress up, a simple sheath probably won't make you happy, no matter how fine the fabric or how much your best friend loves it on you.

Where fantasy meets reality, where fashion meets physique, there is a unique collection of traits that add up to personal style. Here, we offer six bridal archetypes. Hopefully you'll rec-ognize yourself in at least one of them.

Define Your Wedding Style

1. The Timeless Traditionalist

Classic style that never goes out of fashion is what suits this quintessential bride. She avoids trends and instead takes the aisle in a gown that might someday be worn by her own daughter. She will most definitely include something old, something new, something borrowed, and something blue in her ensemble. In fact, the Timeless Traditionalist is happiest if she's wearing something significant that belonged to her ancestors, such as her mother's pearls or her grandmother's gloves.

- Key words: classic, refined, tasteful, enduring.
- Appropriate for formal and semiformal weddings, day or evening.
- Look for designs by Amsale, Anne Barge, Amelia Carrara, Christos, Diamond, Richard Glasgow, Jim Hjelm Couture, Peter Langner, Ron LoVece, Marissa, Alvina Valente.

True story: When Jennifer Aniston and Brad Pitt tied the knot in July 2000, Jennifer outfitted herself in a timelessly traditional way. She wore a full-length gown fashioned of silk and satin and decorated with glass-beaded embroidery. Her ensemble was topped by a crown of pearls and Swarovski crystals, from which cascaded a circular veil.

2. The Princess Bride

It's a fairy-tale wedding, and at its center is a bride in a ball gown who looks as if she just stepped out of a golden carriage drawn by six white horses. This unabashedly feminine bride loves the fantasy of it all and is delighted to play the part of a gossamer creature who might just sprout wings at any moment. Note: Some Princess Brides choose to adopt their look from history and might take the aisle in a Renaissance- or Edwardian-inspired gown or perhaps an antique or vintage accessory.

- Key words: romantic, frothy, historical.
- Appropriate for formal, semiformal, and some informal weddings, day or evening.
- Look for designs by Amelia Casablanca, Eve of Milady, Lazaro, Justina McCaffrey, Candice Solomon, Daniel Thompson, Louise Hamlin Wright.

True story: When actress Traci Bingham (of *Baywatch* fame) planned her 1998 wedding to musician Robb Vallier, she was inspired by three princesses: Princess Grace, Princess Diana, and Cinderella. Her fairy tale came true in a white duchesse satin gown with a seven-layer skirt of embroidered tulle decorated with silk roses. The dress featured a pearled and beaded bodice and a ten-foot train. Framing Traci's face was a vintage diamond tiara and a pair of diamond earrings, which no doubt sparkled extra brightly when she and her husband cut their five-tiered cake.

3. Earth Angel

She doesn't need fussy details or decorative embellishments to feel like a bride. The Earth Angel lets her truest beauty shine through in a soft, graceful gown that moves with her as she floats, flirts, and dances. Comfort is an issue: this bride wants to feel as relaxed as possible on her wedding day. And perhaps she'll accessorize her gown with a bouquet of fresh herbs.

- Key words: unconstructed, flowing, fluid, simple, natural, pure.
- Appropriate for semiformal and informal events, day or evening.
- Look for designs by Amarildine, Christiana Couture, Elizabeth Fillmore, Genny, Amy Kuschel, Manolo, Amy Michelson, Reva Mivasgar, Ristarose.

True story: Cindy Crawford could have worn any gown she wanted on her wedding day. But clothing was low on her list of priorities. She married friend-turned-beau Rande Gerber on the beach in the Bahamas and chose a short, white, slip-type dress for the ceremony. She asked her stylist to make her hair look the way she wished it did when she got out of bed, and she wore a Valentino wrap as a veil. "Beautiful and simple" was the theme; the bride carried a bouquet of sweet peas, and the couple's modest invitation read, "No shoes."

4. The Sophisticate

Anything but girlish and giddy, this bride makes her entrance in an outfit that looks more like an elegant ensemble than a wedding gown. She'll don a smart suit, a brilliantly cut dress, or a minimalist sheath in any length she chooses and make a statement that might resonate from here to Paris and back.

- Key words: chic, dramatic, fashion forward, sleek.
- Appropriate for some formal occasions, plus semiformal and informal affairs.
- Look for designs by Reem Acra, Edgardo Bonilla, Caroline Castigliano, Carolina Herrera, Monique Lhuiller, Badgley Mischka, Helen Morley, Tomasina, Vera Wang, Ritva Westenius.

True story: The day that Carolyn Bessette exchanged "I do's" with John F. Kennedy Jr., wedding gown styles took a quantum leap not seen since Lady Di joined the house of Windsor. Bessette's sleek, understated gown, draped perfectly across her slender frame, became the very definition of the nineties bride. She proved that less can indeed be more, and countless willowy brides continue to follow her impeccable lead.

5. Downtown Girl

She's on the cutting edge of so many things—so why shouldn't she invent her own look for her own day? The Downtown Girl is an informed risk taker who ignores traditional offerings in favor of inventive ones. Whether it's dangerously stylish or dramatically elegant, her look is nothing if not original—and likely years ahead of the runway shows.

- Key words: artistic, modern, unconventional.
- Appropriate for semiformal and informal events, day or evening.
- Look for designs by Domo Adami, Robert Danes, David Fielden, Amanda Wakeley.

True story: Back in the eighties, fashion editor Elizabeth Saltzman was married in New York's Puck Building. Avant-garde designer Stephen Sprouse had created her wedding gown. After the ceremony he approached the bride with a pair of scissors and shortened the gown, which she wore for the rest of the evening.

6. Drama Queen

This bride goes to extremes to make an impression. She'll borrow cultural references from all over the globe, or wear a dress with a silhouette more exciting than the Manhattan skyline, or take her vows in a gown embellished with colorful details. Fabulous hats, fascinating hairdos, surprising hues—all are irresistible to the Drama Queen.

- Key words: avant-garde, eclectic, theatrical, creative.
- Look for designs by Endrius, Eva Haynal Forsythe, Guzzo, Ian Stuart, Beverly Summers.

True story: Perhaps nobody will ever outdo Celine Dion's vow renewal ceremony, held in Las Vegas and featuring a "Thousand and One Nights" theme, complete with camels, exotic birds, and belly dancers (the bride wore a gold caftan by Givenchy). But sometimes drama is in the details: for her Scottish Highlands wedding, Madonna wore a $30,000 Stella McCartney dress in embroidered, off-white satin, accessorized with a tartan sash and topped with a Princess Grace–style tiara. Underneath it all, the Material Mom sported a pair of diamond-studded cowboy boots.

As you're thinking through these preliminary, big-picture questions, make a vow to be true to your style. Everyone, from your best friend to your future mother-in-law, will have an idea of how you should look. But it's what you envision—and ultimately what feels right to you—that should rule the day. Remember, you are the queen of your wedding, and your sovereign word is law.

Chapter Two

Narrow It Down

HOW TO SPEAK
FLUENT WEDDING DRESS

It has been said that there are only three important choices a woman has to make for her wedding: the dress, the location, and the guy. We can't help with the last two, but we can steer you toward a dress that makes you look and feel fabulous.

Hopefully, you've already decided on your wedding style and know what type of bride you are, and are ready to take on the vast and ever-changing subject of wedding gown design. Before you start, you should understand that the bridal industry is based primarily on tradition. Most available gown designs are 1) long—that is, floor length or close to it; 2) white or off-white; and 3) detailed with lace, pearls, beads, crystals, embroideries, sequins, or all six.

So where does that leave you, the bride-to-be, who just

wants to find a great dress that looks good on her? On the one hand, you're blessed, because with these limited parameters the demand for gorgeous gowns keeps inspiring top-notch designers to create spectacular wedding dresses, season after season. On the other hand, you're subject to fierce competition. Celebrity brides with unlimited funds and professionally sculpted bodies are routinely splashed across the pages of magazines, while artistically gifted brides take the Martha Stewart route and handcraft everything from the invitations to the headpiece.

Let them inspire you. Then ignore them. This is about you and your personal journey into the land of the wedding gown, where you will learn to identify styles, colors, lengths, fabrics, necklines, and more. You'll come to know the universe of options available to you and decide what you like and what you loathe. Then, you'll match your body type with the style of dress that highlights your assets and downplays your imperfections. Finally, you'll pitch fantasy against reality and catch your perfect dress at the crossroads.

SILHOUETTE

As far as bridal consultants are concerned, the silhouette is where the dress discussions begin. Flattery matters: certain gown shapes are fundamentally suited to specific bodies, and it's the consultant's job to make a love match between a bride and her best look. Though it seems as if silhouettes are reinvented every season, there are classic shapes that are the industry standards.

Your basic glossary of bridal gown silhouettes:

Narrow It Down

A-line or princess: This statuesque, gently flared gown features vertical panels that descend either from the shoulders or from under the bust to form a slim shape that widens gradually toward the hem. The A-line/princess silhouette is considered to be universally flattering. Says Dorothy Silver, director of merchandising and sales at Kleinfeld: "A-line is probably the number one dress shape for any body type, whether big, tall, petite, or slim."

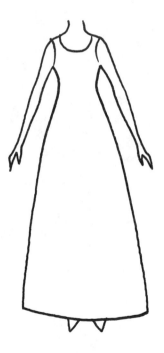

Ball gown: With a fitted, corset-type bodice and a dramatically full skirt, this gown might feature a waistline that is natural (at your actual waistline), basque (dropping to a V shape slightly below your waist), or dropped (hugging the top of your hips). If you're not in love with your hips, buttocks, or legs, the ball gown is a fine disguise. At Kleinfeld, certain highly embellished ball gown styles are referred to as "fantasy" or "Cinderella" dresses.

Narrow It Down

Empire: The upper body is showcased by this high-waisted silhouette, which features a snug bosom and a skirt that cascades into a gentle column or a fuller skirt. It's usually a long, slim gown that features a variety of necklines and can be sleeveless or with short sleeves. This style tends to suit women who have medium to large busts and less-than-perfect waistlines.

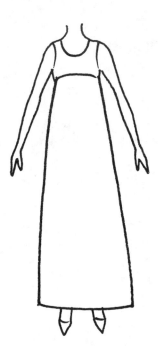

Mermaid: A body-hugging sheath that flares at or below the knee to create a fluttering flamenco-like hemline.

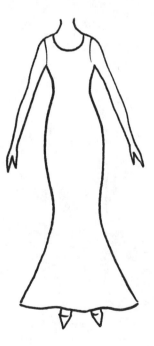

Narrow It Down

Sheath: Simple and chic, this minimalist style borrows from evening gown design and usually follows the body's curves from top to bottom. Some sheaths are cut on the bias, which causes them to cling in a most revealing way. Director of administration and sales Roseann Clerkin says that contemporary sheaths have been very popular. "Plain slip dresses, bias cut, backless, no embellishments . . . they're sexy as can be, and most of the brides who are buying them have dynamite bodies."

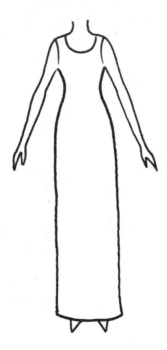

A QUESTION OF COLOR

Dear Bride-to-Be: You don't have to be a virgin to wear white. That tradition—and its corresponding myth—was started less than two hundred years ago when Queen Victoria married Prince Albert. She wore white as a symbol of purity. Before that, brides of the British empire (and beyond) were married in their best dresses, no matter what color they happened to be. As late as 1928, American fashion magazines described wedding gowns made of ivory satin decorated with tiny green leaves; pale yellow georgette with pink tulle veiling; and "wedding slippers" fashioned from silver brocade.

In many countries—including Africa, India, China, and Japan—it is believed that vibrant colors bring blessings to newly joined couples. Brides in the United States are now starting to step away from white and getting married in colors that simply make them happy. Actress Sharon Stone wore pink for her 1998 wedding to Phil Bronstein; actress Elizabeth Perkins wore a bronze gown when she married Julio Macat in 2000.

Though color horizons are slowly expanding, the majority of brides-to-be in this country still prefer white or shades of white for their dress of the day. According to Lara Westock, the bridal manager at Kleinfeld, by far the most popular colors for bridal gowns are white and ivory. "I would say it's about sixty-forty," she says, with most of the brides choosing silk white over ivory or off-white. "A lot of older brides are worried about wearing pure white," adds bridal consultant Sadie Mandane. She says they often choose off-white shades like candlelight or champagne.

The difference between "stark white" and "champagne" may be broader than you imagine; the following terminology will help you hone in on the shade that's right for you.

Stark white: As white as an aspirin, with subtle overtones of blue, this intense shade is only available in synthetic fabrics and can be strikingly beautiful on dark-skinned women.

Natural white, silk white, diamond white: These true whites are warmer and creamier than stark white. Associated with natural fibers (silk, cotton, linen, and so on), they tend to be flattering to fair-skinned brides.

Ivory, eggshell, candlelight: This group of off-white shades with golden undertones can resemble anything from pasteurized milk to frozen custard. Choose carefully within this category; your skin might look divine against one designer's idea of candlelight and pasty against another's.

Champagne, rum: These off-white colors have pink undertones that particularly flatter brides with dark or olive-toned complexions.

GREAT LENGTHS

Karen Duffy, former MTV deejay and author of *Model Patient,* eloped in a dress so short that, out of respect for her parents and in-laws, she had her wedding photos airbrushed to make it look longer. On the other hand, actress Angela Bassett got married in an Escada gown with a four-foot-long French lace train.

The gown length you choose has much to do with your wedding style. Formal ceremonies call for longer dresses (floor length preferred), while informal events allow for all kinds of flexibility. Standard options include the following:

Narrow It Down

Floor length: Hemline is ½ inch to 1½ inches from the floor. This is the traditional choice for formal weddings.

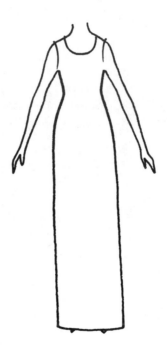

Ballerina length: Usually associated with wide, poufed skirts, the ballerina hemline falls just above the ankle.

Narrow It Down

Tea length: Generally paired with slim silhouettes, tea-length dresses end at the lower calf or above the ankle.

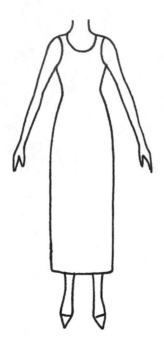

Intermission length: Longer in back, shorter in front.

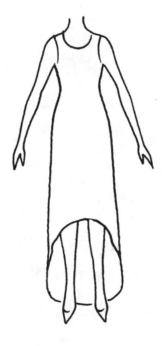

Narrow It Down

Asymmetrical: Longer on one side than the other.

Street length: A hemline that falls just below the knee.

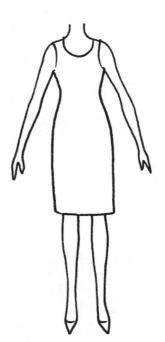

Narrow It Down

Mini: This leg-showcasing length can fall anywhere from right above the knee to just this side of shocking.

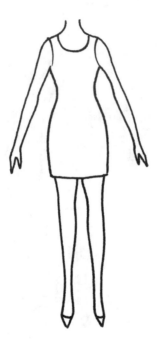

EXPRESSIVE NECKLINES

Wedding gown necklines are more powerful than you might think: besides being essential to the structure and the style of the dress, the neckline provides a sort of miniature staging area for the chest, shoulders, neck, and especially the bride's face.

Your neckline options include the following:

Off-the-shoulder: This low-slung neckline dips below the collarbone and extends on each side to a point below the shoulders. It may feature full-length sleeves or just a band that hugs the upper arms. A more extreme version of the off-the-shoulder look, the portrait neckline extends horizontally across the body from upper arm to upper arm, leaving the shoulders completely bare.

Bertha: A variation of the off-the-shoulder and portrait styles is the "Bertha collar," a wide, deep collar that exposes the shoulders and meets under the bustline.

Sweetheart: This distinctive neckline begins about two inches inside the shoulder line and dips to a heart shape at the bustline. The sweetheart neckline tends to accentuate cleavage to the extent that the chest is sometimes covered in sheer netting or any other translucent fabric; in that case it's known as an "illusion" neckline. Another variation is the Queen Anne, a high-standing collar that curves down to a sweetheart front.

Bateau: Extends horizontally from one shoulder to another, gently following the curve of the collarbone. A variation of the bateau is the Sabrina, which cuts a straight line from shoulder to shoulder.

Halter: This evening-wear staple is best known as a low-cut style in which two panels of fabric are attached at the waistline or under the bust and meet at the nape of the neck in a clasp, collar, or tie. Halter necklines can also be fashioned from a solid front panel that fastens at the back of the neck.

Scoop: A rounded neckline. Beginning at the shoulders, a scoop might dip below the collarbone, above the bustline, or somewhere in between.

Jewel: Also known as a "T-shirt" neckline, this rounded cut circles the base of the neck.

Square: A rectangle or half-square neckline. Some square cuts extend clear to the shoulder line, giving the illusion that the gown's sleeves are separate from the dress.

Keyhole: A cutout that reveals a circle of skin. The classic keyhole neckline fastens at the neck and has a cutout beneath.

Surplice: A neckline in which one panel of fabric overlaps and either ties around or is attached at the waist.

V-neck: As the name implies, this neckline features a pointed plunge. It can be as subtle as a decorative nick in the upper edge of a corset bodice or as spectacular as a deep, cleavage-baring plunge.

Sleeveless: A gown is considered sleeveless if 1) it has no sleeves; and 2) its back attaches to its front at the shoulders. Though this may seem like an obvious definition, the line between "sleeveless" and "strapless" can be faint. What if a dress has a stiff bodice that could easily stay up on its own yet features decorative straps? It's still considered sleeveless, not strapless. So is the halter-top gown, whose front and back pieces attach to a collar, and the wispy, slip-style gown with straps so slender that they make strands of spaghetti feel fat.

Strapless: Describes any style that leaves the neck and shoulders completely bare; today most strapless gowns feature structured bodices. "Strapless is our number one neckline," says Tina Gatto, Kleinfeld's assistant bridal manager. "It gives the most comfort. You can dance wildly in it, and the way we fit our dresses, you're not going to have to pull it up all night."

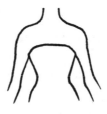

Crumb catcher: Not technically a neckline style, this is a decorative insert of fabric at or above the bustline. The crumb catcher originated in medieval times, before napkins were invented. Ladies of the court wore gowns that had a piece of fabric that protruded from the top of the bodice. Its job: to catch crumbs, of course. Today the crumb catcher is usually seen on the front and/or back of a dress as a lovely detail.

THE BACK STORY

Backlines have become increasingly important over the years, especially with the current popularity of slinky, body-conscious bridal wear. As a bride, you should pay special attention to that oft-neglected expanse between the nape of your neck and the arch of your back: on the day of your wedding, it will be showcased on the aisle, at the altar, on the dance floor, at the cake cutting, during the bouquet toss . . . you get the picture.

Backlines are a favorite playground of top designers, and why not? Among fashion-centric brides there is a strong demand for gowns that are unembellished and which rely on cut, fabric, and drape to make a statement. The backs of these contemporary gowns provide a sort of blank canvas; they can be made sexy, revealing, and/or ultrastylish without compromising a bride's desire for understated chic.

Trendy new backlines are introduced every season and are added to the array of established backline styles that have complemented gowns—and the brides who wear them—for decades.

Scoop: This rounded backline curves from shoulder to shoulder in a half-circle or oval shape. Scoop backs can be modest (dipping just below the shoulder line) or dramatic (reaching to the waist or beyond) and can be found on all sorts of dresses, including bias-cut sheaths and fancy ball gowns.

Backless: This gown exposes a broad expanse of back, with barely a trace of visual support. Halter dresses and contemporary, body-clinging gowns are most likely to be backless and might dare to dip below the small of the back. When a gown is cut dramatically low both in the front and the back, Kleinfeld bridal consultants wryly refer to it as "a double-cleavage dress."

Narrow It Down

Surplice: This backline features two panels of fabric that overlap onto one another and either wrap and tie at the waist or are stitched to the waistline.

Keyhole: A cutout in front or, most commonly, in back that teasingly exposes a section of flesh. The classic keyhole back fastens at the nape of the neck and has a circular or oval cutout beneath, which can be as small as a silver dollar or large enough to render a dress virtually backless.

Illusion: An illusion insert occurs when the exposed area is covered with a translucent fabric such as netting, tulle, or lace.

THE BRIDAL BODICE

In medieval Europe, bodices were stiff, vestlike outergarments that laced up the front and were worn over shapeless dresses to give definition to the waist and bust.

Today, the word *bodice* defines that portion of a dress that covers the torso, including the bust, the waist, and, in some instances, the hips. This is the part of the wedding gown that will define—or perhaps disguise—your upper body. Often, successful dress shopping begins with the search for the right bodice style.

Basic bodice styles include the following:

Corset: When most people hear the word *bodice,* the corset style is what they're thinking of: a smooth, structured, torso hugger, often strapless and usually paired with a voluminous skirt. Many corset bodices are supported by metal or plastic bands known as "stays" or "bones"; others maintain their shape with an inner layer of stiff fabric. Although some corsets have lacing that snakes up the front or the back, just as in

merry old England, the majority have flat-panel fronts that are perfectly suited to decorative embellishments such as embroidery, beading, appliqués, feathers, or fur. Modern corset styles vary in length and can fall at the natural waistline, drop below the waistline, or descend into a V shape at the abdomen, a style known as a "basque" waistline. Neckline and backline options are many, and so are sleeve styles, but most contemporary corset-topped gowns are sleeveless or strapless.

Empire: A classic style with a waistline situated directly under the bust. Empire dresses usually have low-cut necklines, distinctive backlines, and graceful, slim skirts. This type of gown was worn by the empress Josephine when she married Napoleon Bonaparte, but she wasn't the first: her wedding dress was adapted from an ancient Roman design. In fact, the word *empire* is a reference to the Roman empire.

Halter: The quintessential halter is both a bodice and a neckline, fashioned from split panels that are attached, at the front, to a waistband of sorts and connected in a clasp at the nape of the neck. Some modern halters feature a single panel of fabric in the front, which might be softly gathered at or just below the waist to create a subtle blouson effect. Though bare backs are a hallmark of the halter-topped gown, some designers feature cutout backs, surplice sashes, and T backs.

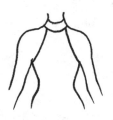 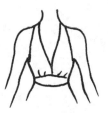

One-shoulder: These asymmetrical dresses showcase one arm that dares to be bare and another that's demurely dressed. The single sleeve can be long or short. The dress can also be sleeveless.

Princess: This style follows the shape of the upper body. Vertical panels descend in an A-line from either the shoulders or just beneath the bust.

Tank: A sleeveless bodice that resembles a tank top in shape, complete with substantial straps and dropped, scooped armholes. A tank can be a separate top paired with a skirt or a one-piece dress. Structured, corset-type bodices can also be found in the tank style.

THE MEANING OF SLEEVES

Sleeves present designers with a great opportunity for artistic expression. Long, linear, and almost always in motion, arms are irresistible models for all kinds of sleeve styles, from romantic to risqué.

Cap: A short, fitted sleeve that just covers the shoulders. When paired with a corset-style top, cap sleeves can look almost as if they're detached from the bodice.

Tulip: A short, set-in sleeve with overlapping fabric. The tulip is usually seen as an extension of a scoop or sweetheart neckline.

Balloon: A voluminous sleeve that puffs out from the shoulder to as far as the wrist. One variation is the "pouf," which is a short gathered sleeve that can be worn on or off the shoulder.

Fitted: A sleeve with little or no fullness. One variation is the "fitted point," a long sleeve that ends in a V shape that drapes over the top of the hand.

Juliet: A long sleeve with a poufed shoulder and a fitted lower arm.

Leg-o'-mutton: A long sleeve that's full from the shoulder to just above the elbow. It's similar to the "bishop" sleeve, which is gathered at the shoulder and fitted from below the elbow to the cuff.

Poet: A sleeve that ends in ruffles or pleats. The length sometimes extends all the way to the fingertips.

Bell: Narrow at the top, this long sleeve flares out at its bottom edge.

Warning:
Long Sleeves Have Their Limitations!

If your fiancé is much taller than you, beware of choosing a gown with long, fitted sleeves. "You won't be able to raise your arms over your head," warns Nitsa Glezelis, who is director of alterations at Kleinfeld. In fact, she adds, "You probably won't be able to raise your arms any higher than your shoulders." This means that, unless your groom is shorter than you, you can't throw your arms around his neck, whether it's for a kiss or your first dance. "Brides can usually work around the problem," says Nitsa, "but it usually means hugging the husband around his waist."

PS: If you decide on wearing long, fitted sleeves, keep Nitsa's words in mind when it comes time to toss your bouquet.

Narrow It Down

Your Right to Bare Arms

Do you love the dress but hate the sleeves? Don't cross it off your list: sleeves are perhaps the most fluid of all bridal dress details, and many can be altered, adjusted, or removed altogether. Brides who require long sleeves for religious reasons might also be able to choose a sleeveless gown style and have sleeves added on. The point is don't be too quick to rule out a dress you otherwise love because you're not mad about the sleeves. You may just be able to mix and match the sleeves you want with the dress that has you under its spell.

THE POETRY OF FABRICS

Much of a wedding dress's artistry is best expressed in the texture, drape, and movement of its fabrics. Historically, sumptuous, costly textiles were an important part of wedding rituals, because they signified the prosperity of the bride's family. Today, modern textile techniques and advances in the quality of synthetic blends can make a bride look rich even if she isn't. Other than silk itself, all the fabric types described below are available in silk or synthetic blends. Following are the top choices of bridal designers:

Silk: Fiber made from silkworm cocoons. Silk fabric comes in many different varieties, including shantung, duchesse, zymboline, and mikado.

Satin: A heavy, tightly woven fabric that's glossy on the front and dull on the back.

Organza: A sheer fabric more flowing than tulle but stiffer than chiffon. A favorite choice for multilayered skirts.

Taffeta: A crisp, lustrous fabric with a papery feel.

Tulle: A netting made of silk, nylon, or rayon. Tulle can be soft (as seen on veils or poufed ballerina skirts) or stiff (used in layers under skirts to give them body and volume).

Narrow It Down

Charmeuse: A lightweight, semilustrous fabric with a soft texture.

Chiffon: A delicate, semitransparent fabric with a soft finish. Most often seen layered on skirts or veils.

Linen: A fabric woven from flax. It's cooler than cotton but tends to wrinkle easily.

Brocade: A heavy, intricately woven fabric with three-dimensional designs.

Damask: Similar to brocade, with designs expressed in texture.

Illusion: Although not made of one specific fabric, this fine, translucent netting usually seen on neck panels, back panels, or sheer sleeves.

LOVE TRAINS

Bridal trains come in two basic styles. A detachable train is an optional panel of fabric that attaches to the gown at the back of the waist and trails behind the bride. The second style is part of the skirt itself, a luxurious expanse of fabric that prettily extends from the rear sweep of the gown and needs to be "bustled"—that is, gathered up via a series of tiny hooks, snaps, or bows so that the bride can get in and out of limos and move freely throughout her reception. Long trains are considered more formal than shorter trains, with the cathedral and monarch lengths reserved for the most formal affairs.

"Trains are never out of style," asserts Judith Lerner, who has been a Kleinfeld bridal consultant for eighteen years. "Some girls want them, some don't—it's a matter of a bride's personal taste." Judith notes that very few designers offer detachable trains as part of a gown, but such trains can be custom made at a bride's request—and embellished with monograms or other special details.

Narrow It Down

Sweep: This short train might barely touch the floor.

Court: A modest yet formal train that extends up to three feet from the hem of the gown.

Narrow It Down

Chapel: Generally the most popular length for fancy affairs, this train extends 3½ to 4½ feet from the hemline.

Cathedral: A formal train that extends 6½ to 8 feet from the waist.

Extended cathedral, royal cathedral, monarch: The most dramatic of trains, these can measure anywhere from nine to twelve feet from the waist . . . or more.

Watteau: A train that attaches to the back of the shoulders or the top of a strapless dress.

BASIC TRAINING

Nicole Losurdo, Kleinfeld's accessory manager, knows a thing or two about trains. Her advice: "Trains are romantic. Brides can wear them during the ceremony, then hold them during the first dance. But after that, a train has got to be bustled! Otherwise people will step on it all night." Nicole says that trains can almost always be lengthened or shortened by request. Custom-made trains are also available, but she warns that some fabrics and gown styles aren't trainworthy. "We can't do a train on a bias-cut dress," she asserts. That's because the fabric for these dresses is cut at an angle and so the fabric itself doesn't provide the width that a train requires.

Nicole's final bit of advice: Mud and trains don't mix. "Trains might not be right for garden weddings," she says, "or any event that takes place outdoors."

The Personal Train

Some brides choose to have their trains embroidered with a monogram, family crest, or other meaningful motif. Such embellishments are a nice touch, since most couples have their backs to their assembled loved ones during the ceremony.

One recent Kleinfeld client wanted to have an enormous letter B—her fiancé's initial—embroidered on her train in crystal beads. It required a very long train, which the beading department draped across ten or so tables. Eyewitnesses reported that when the bride walked down the aisle, she looked like the Queen Bee.

ELEGANT EMBELLISHMENTS

Some brides-to-be shudder at the word *embellishment.* Perhaps they fear the idea of a perfectly good wedding gown being covered up by sequins and beading, turning it from gorgeous to garish. In fact, wedding gown embellishments can be both tasteful and genuinely pretty, and often it is the intimate details—a ribbon here, a crystal there—that make a dress really special.

Here's everything you wanted to know about embellishments but were afraid to ask:

Appliqués: These are fabric cutouts that are sewn onto the dress. Often the cutouts themselves are embellished by embroidery, beading, or sequins.

Beading: Tiny beads made of polished glass, crystal, metal, gems, or other materials are sewed (or sometimes, unfortunately, glued) onto the dress, usually in a border pattern, spot pattern, or overall pattern. Bugle beads are cylindrical and lend themselves to edgings and curved designs. Austrian crystals, made from polished and faceted lead crystal, are especially popular: some are clear, while others, known as "AB" crystals, are iridescent and reflect full-spectrum light.

Colored beads are appearing more often on today's gowns. Kleinfeld beading manager Penny Touranont has seen an increased demand for designs rendered in pink, lavender, silver, and gold. Rarely does a bride request blazing expanses of strong hues. Usually it's "just little touches here and there," says Penny.

Monia Marceca, a bridal consultant at Kleinfeld, notes that more designers are showing white gowns accented with splashes of color. "Some have blue beading, some have pink," she says. "We also see green and multicolors, especially if it's a flower motif."

Edging: These border accents range from braids, ribbons, and ruffles to narrow strips of lace, embroidery, beadwork, or fringe.

Embroidery: Whether hand-sewn or made by machine, embroidery turns mere thread into leaves, flowers, patterns, and monograms, and can range from full-skirt masterpieces to tiny border accents. Though bridal embroidery is traditionally white on white, some newer dresses are embroidered with contrasting colors, including red and orange.

Exotic embellishments: The bride with a taste for unconventional accents might cast her eye toward dyed-to-match fur, seashells, velvet leaves, silk flowers, or feather boas with quivering tendrils.

Jewels: Some progressive brides are choosing to integrate faux jewels—including rhinestones, synthetic emeralds, near rubies, and pretend sapphires—on bodices, skirts, or any part of a wedding gown that might usually be embellished by beads or pearls. Jewels are also being used as sparkling accents on veils and illusion netting across the back or chest.

Lace: Though some skirts and bodices are entirely overlaid by lace, more often lace is used as an accent on sleeves, necklines, and hems. There are dozens of popular styles of lace, including Alençon, the soft and intricate Chantilly; the heavy, braid-enhanced Battenberg; and the whispery point d'esprit, which is little more than subtle patterns of dots on a net background.

Alençon, The Queen of Lace

In pre-Napoleonic Europe, all lace was produced by hand in Italy and Flanders. Fine lace was so valued that, when Napoleon came to power in France, he assigned spies to infiltrate those countries to learn the secret of lace making. His intelligence gathering led to the development of a light, airy lace made of linen thread. Called Alençon (ah-lawn-son)—named for the town in Normandy, France where it was perfected—it became the most pricey and coveted lace in the world, and France soon outpaced both Italy and Flanders in lace production. Eventually, machines took the place of French needlepoint artisans, yet Alençon remains the "queen of lace" to this day.

Narrow It Down

Pearls: The smallest are seed pearls, applied singly or in strands to give texture and richness to gowns, veils, and trains. Baroque pearls are irregularly shaped and thus lend a slightly more organic look to decorative areas. Like wedding gowns themselves, pearls are most often seen in shades of white and off-white, though silver-toned pearls make an appearance now and then.

Sequins: Highly reflective, these plastic disks—each no larger than a raindrop—twinkle magically both indoors and out. Like beading and other shiny embellishments, they reflect movement as well as light.

Fringe Benefits

In her autobiography, legendary fashionista Diana Vreeland exclaims, "How I miss fringe!" Indeed, once the staple of irrepressible flappers and hippies in suede vests, fringe adds movement to garments and seems to come into vogue whenever the reigning establishment needs shaking up. It's not often seen on wedding gowns, though Vreeland herself caused a minor scandal among New York socialites when she wore a white dress dripping with fringe to her coming-out party in 1923.

ONE GOWN
THREE DISTINCT LOOKS

Virtually every successful wedding gown is a product of collaboration. The designer establishes the look, which is dependent on structure, style, fabric, drape, and lots of other crucial elements that make the dress the Dress. But because most gowns are made to order, there is a substantial window of opportunity that allows the bride (with the help of a consultant or other bridal professional) to customize the dress to her liking. Though she can't reinvent the wheel, she can make a number of design choices that might dramatically affect the final product.

Customizing a wedding dress is a process of addition and subtraction. If you adore the shape of a dress but are turned off by its bows, beading, and ruffles, go ahead and order the dress without the decorative details. On the other hand, if you've found the gown of your dreams but can't imagine walking down the aisle in anything less than a cathedral-length train, make your wishes known and work out a way to make them come true.

Look at the three dresses below, each a customized version of the same basic dress. Dress 1 features sheer sleeves, with embroidery that matches the embroidery on the bodice, and a satin skirt with a flat front panel and soft side pleating. Dress 2 shows the sheer sleeves removed to make it a strapless dress. Dress 3 brings back the sheer sleeves and turns the satin skirt into a full, princess tulle skirt. One dress, three distinct looks.

Narrow It Down

Dress 1

Dress 2

Dress 3

Custom orders might cost you more time and money, but the last thing you want to feel on your wedding day is a sense of regret. Don't settle for anything less than true love.

YOUR BODY, YOUR SELF

One of the lovely things about wedding gowns is that they're designed for real women. There is no "perfect body" in the bridal industry; when it comes to finding the right dress, willowy model types have no particular advantage over full-figured five-footers. Gowns are created in a stunning variety of styles, and each is looking for a figure to flatter.

When searching for a shape and a drape that's right for you, first you must know yourself. Not just your inner self, but your basic body type. Though you're probably a pro at finding regular clothes that highlight your assets and minimize your less-perfect features, there's a big difference between choosing the right cut of jeans and zeroing in on the gown that will make you look gorgeous today, tomorrow, and all the years that your wedding portrait rests on your mantel.

Kleinfeld bridal consultant Dyan Bonjourno knows all about making matches between body types and wedding gowns. "Everybody wants to look thinner," says the seven-year bridal industry veteran. "The itty-bitty girls are most obsessed about it—the size fours want to look like ones." Yet not every bride knows what looks best on her body. "You may have a size eighteen girl who would be best in an A-line shape. But from the time she was five, when she got a Barbie in a big tulle skirt, that's what she's wanted to wear." How does Dyan deal with the bride whose heart is set on an unflattering style? "I bring it to her, I let her look at herself in the mirror. If she says, 'It's not me,' then I direct her toward the A-line area."

Dyan admits that gown shopping isn't easy for larger-size brides. "Dresses are little to begin with," she says. "In the real world, I'm about a size eight. I wear about a size twelve wedding gown, and lots of times the proportions aren't as cute in the plus sizes. But it depends on the dress. Some dresses are just as beautiful big."

Petite brides have their own special challenges. "I see a lot of 'too much dress, not enough bride,'" says Dianne Barbaro, Kleinfeld's bridal consultant. "Sometimes the dress is wearing the girl, especially if she's petite." When embellishments and design details threaten to swamp a bride, Dianne steps forward. "I say, 'You're too pretty for this dress.' You don't want to miss the face and end up looking at all this stuff!"

In the world of bridal wear, size doesn't matter. But shape does. There are women who have curvy proportions, meaning that their busts and/or hips are noticeably wider than their waists, while other women are built more like classical columns, with little definition among their upper, middle, and lower bodies. Even if the curvy woman and the columnar woman wear the same size, the dresses that flatter them are very different in shape.

When assessing your own proportions, cross-reference the following pointers. Hopefully you'll find a style that makes the most of what you've got.

Great Heights

The laws for dressing short or tall brides aren't carved in stone, because so much depends on the height-weight ratio. Here are some suggestions, each open to interpretation.

If you want to look taller:

- Go for a gown with long, uninterrupted lines, such as a sheath or a mermaid style. If your body isn't quite right for those form-fitting options, try an A-line, princess, or Empire-cut dress.
- High necklines add length. Depending on your body shape, however, they might also add width.
- Gowns with fitted waists and full skirts can cut shorter women in half (visually, of course) and make them look undersized. There is a two-part solution, in case you're in this category and have your heart set on a Cinderella ball gown: 1) choose a dress with a basque-waisted bodice that ends in a V at your lower tummy line; and 2) wear the highest heels you can stand.
- Don't bog yourself down with details. Beading, embroidery, ribbons, and/or lace should be limited to the chest and shoulder areas.

- Consider a dress or suit that's tea length, street length, or mini. Many a delicate-boned bride is overwhelmed by the sheer volume of a traditional wedding dress; you might find your future in a sweet little slip dress that skims the top of your knees or a stylish skirt suit with a waist-length jacket.

To downplay your height:

- Try low-cut or strapless gowns with full skirts.
- Go for horizontal details, including neckbands, necklaces, panels around the bust or waist, belted or sashed waistlines, or skirts with various-length layers.
- Halter-top styles can be great on tall women with strongly defined shoulder areas, especially if the halter attaches at the waist.
- Avoid design elements that elongate the body, such as Empire waists, dropped waists, and sheath-type gowns that fall in an uninterrupted line from top to bottom.
- Feel free to experiment with different skirt lengths, including ankle-length and tea-length.

It's a Bust

The average adult American female wears a size 36C bra. It's an interesting statistic, but once again, size is only relative. If you're five feet tall and weigh 104 pounds, a 36C bust is prodigious; if, on the other hand, you're five eleven and a muscular

180, that same bust size might appear to be smaller than average. In any case, whether you're an A cup or a double-D, bust size can easily be enhanced or downplayed with a combination of the right undergarments and the appropriate style of gown.

The bride with a generous bustline should:

- Look for off-the-shoulder, sweetheart, Queen Anne, scoop, strapless, square-cut, or V-shaped necklines with minimal embellishments. These styles flatter medium to large busts without adding weight to the rest of the body whether you choose to display cleavage or not.
- Avoid high, closed necklines such as the jewel, the bateau, or the wedding collar, which can make larger breasts look low and ponderous.
- Steer clear of dress styles that make breast support a problem, including the portrait neckline, the unstructured tank bodice, halter-tops and backless styles.
- Visually diminish large bustlines by giving more width to the lower body via wide and/or dramatic skirts.
- Keep the neck area unobstructed (for example, avoid conspicuous necklaces or chokers).

The petite-busted bride might:

- Shop for Sabrina, bateau, or jewel necklines and bodices that are enhanced by overlays, beadwork, or other embellishments.

Narrow It Down

- Look for slim gown styles such as the sheath or the mermaid, which are kind to narrow chests and shoulders.
- Consider the "crumb catcher"—a decorative band of fabric attached to the upper bodice of a dress. Some crumb catchers are made of voluminous fabrics and extend beyond the bodice to encircle the upper arms. Others are simple bands enhanced with beading and embroidery. Either way, they can balance proportions for a most pleasing effect.
- Avoid necklines designed to showcase cleavage (such as the V neck or sweetheart) and dresses that can't be worn with a push-up bra or padded inserts (including many halter and backless styles).

Most medium-busted women can feel confident wearing:

- Scoop, off-shoulder, Empire, V-neck, backless, strapless, halter, Bertha collar, portrait, and square-cut necklines.

Such a Waist!

Wedding gown waistlines have a tremendous amount of power. They can transform a pear shape into an hourglass, make a boyish physique seem positively voluptuous, tame the wildest of hips, and solve lots of figure flaws in between.

To flatter a pear-shaped figure that's smaller above the waist and larger below:

- Combine a decorative neckline and shoulder area with a form-fitting bodice and a full or flared skirt.
- Give substance to narrow shoulders with puffy-sleeve styles such as the Juliet, leg-o'-mutton, bishop, or pouf.

To make the most of a larger bustline and smaller hips (inverted pear shape):

- Try a princess, A-line, or Empire style that is narrow at the shoulders and bust and gradually flares out to a wider hemline.
- Balance proportions by choosing a structured bodice and a voluminous skirt, with little or no decorations above the waist.

If your bust, waist, and hips are virtually the same width:

- Look for full or flared skirts paired with jewel or bateau necklines; fluffy shoulders and/or sleeves; A-line or Empire styles with trains; crumb catcher bustlines; or two-piece ensembles with jackets that end at the lower hip.
- Avoid dress styles that emphasize or define the waistline area.

For hourglass figures (full hips and bust with a small waist) or semihourglass figures (medium bust and hips with a smallish waist):

Narrow It Down

- Try ball gown styles with basque or natural-waist bodice, or virtually any shape of gown with scoop, sweetheart, off-shoulder, V-neck, square, or strapless necklines.
- Look for sheaths or mermaid gowns or halter-top and/or backless styles.

Shoulders and Necklines and Backs, Oh My!

Though there are no fitness gurus on TV making you feel bad about the shape of your back, shoulders, neck, and upper chest, these areas can't be ignored when choosing a dress that flatters. Look at yourself in the mirror: Do you have a strong collarbone, a slender neck, a smooth upper chest, and shoulders that are more or less horizontal? If so, you're a great candidate for necklines that display your uppermost body, such as the scoop, Sabrina, square, strapless, halter, and portrait.

On the other hand, if your shoulders descend from your neckline in a notable slope; your upper chest is disproportionately narrow or concave in shape; the ribs below your collarbone are visible; or you have a plump or thin neck, you should probably downplay these areas with the help of bateau, jewel, and illusion necklines.

Now, check out your back. If your posture is good, your skin is relatively clear, and you like what you see, then it's probably okay for you to wear a back-exposing dress.

How Agatha Got Her Dress

The year was 1997. Brooklyn native Agatha Abitino was engaged to marry Angelo Alicandro. Kleinfeld was the place where Agatha wanted to shop; little did she know that it would become her home away from home

Armed with images clipped from magazines, Agatha went with her mom to her first appointment at Kleinfeld. "I met my bridal consultant," she recalls. "She made me feel so comfortable. I explained what I wanted, and she gave me dresses. . . . It turns out the pictures I brought were really not what I wanted."

With the help of her intuitive consultant, Agatha found her gown—traditional, pretty, ultrafeminine—within five tries. "I knew right away," she says of the dress, which had off-shoulder sleeves and a cathedral-length train. On her second visit, accompanied by additional friends and family members, she ordered the gown in which she was going to be married.

"The next day," Agatha remembers, "I got a phone call from Kleinfeld. It was a manager, and she told me that the gown I'd chosen could not be made in time for my wedding. I was crying and crying. She said, 'Come in, we'll find you what you want.'"

When Agatha returned to Kleinfeld, she was surrounded by helpers and supporters. "They all tried to make me happy," she says. "Sure enough, I found a gown that was just as beautiful." Agatha's replacement dress didn't

Narrow It Down

have a train, however. So the staff offered to create one for her. "I had originally wanted a cathedral train," she says. "But the church I was getting married in had a very long center aisle, so I said, 'Let's make it longer.'" With counseling from Kleinfeld experts, Agatha decided on a monarch-length train measuring a full four yards. It was designed to be detachable, which, she says now, was an excellent idea. "Imagine wearing a train that long at the reception? It would have been impossible."

A train of such grand proportions called for equally grand embellishments. Enter Peggy Touranont, Kleinfeld's beading manager. "She matched the beadwork from the bodice of the dress," says Agatha, "and put it on the train." In order to compete with the extended train and an even longer veil, Agatha's gown needed bolstering. "I wanted my skirt to be more poufy, and they gave me a second crinoline," she says. "They gave me everything I asked for."

Agatha had such a good time at Kleinfeld that she started showing up every Thursday. "I was there constantly," she says, laughing. "Nine times, ten times, just to try my dress on again. I was excited, I wanted to be in that atmosphere and be with the employees and all the other brides. I was there so often, they actually offered me a job."

Agatha Alicandro didn't join the Kleinfeld staff. But she did get married in August of 1998, surrounded by eleven attendants in blush-colored dresses. Agatha says it was the most memorable day of her life—that is, until February 2001, when her baby boy was born. "Now it's my second most memorable day," she says with a smile.

Chapter Three

The Fine Art
of Successful Shopping

Every married woman has a wedding dress story to tell. Tales are swapped at showers and receptions, told with glee over coffee or cocktails, passed down through generations. Once in a while, a story will emerge about a woman who bought the first wedding dress she ever tried on. It fit her perfectly, of course, and looked smashing. She brought it home that very day and never looked back.

Urban legend? Probably. For most brides, shopping for a wedding gown requires forethought, planning, and attention to detail. Think of it: If you were buying a house or starting a business, you wouldn't just blunder into the marketplace and invest in the first thing that caught your eye, would you? Of course not; you'd gather information, call upon advisers, marshal your energies, and set yourself up for success. The same goes for buying your wedding dress.

This chapter is both a blueprint and a tool kit. Full of pointers and shortcuts, it will guide you through the wilds of the wedding gown world so that you may emerge, in a year or so, feeling victorious and looking gorgeous from head to toe.

YOUR SHOPPING SCHEDULE

It's never too early to start shopping for a wedding dress . . . to a point. Though some happily married women claim that it took them longer to find a dress than it did to find a husband, the shopping process should ideally start no earlier than one year before the wedding. That's because fashions can change just enough over the course of a year that you may run the risk of buying "last year's dress." Worse, you might see dresses very similar to yours at every wedding from now until the day you say "I do."

However, you should order your dream dress nine to twelve months before the wedding. Why so much advance time? Because most bridal gowns are custom-made and require as many as four fittings before they can be declared altarworthy. The creation of your dress is a team effort and might involve the contributions of seamstresses, embroiderers, beaders, and other artisans—not to mention fabric suppliers. Then there is that major variable called you. What if you suddenly abhor the neckline of your dress? What if you lose seven pounds before the wedding? If you give yourself plenty of lead time, the salon will have time to fix any manufacturer's mistake.

Timelines are a bride's best friend. Take this one to heart.

Nine to Twelve Months in Advance

- Decide on the date and the general style of your wedding.
- Narrow down your wedding dress options in terms of style and budget (as outlined in chapters 1 and 2).
- Find out if there are going to be any religious requirements that will limit your gown selection. For instance, some places of worship don't allow brides to expose their arms, shoulders, and/or legs.
- Edit your collection of magazine clippings. Only keep pictures of dresses that might actually work for you, and pay attention to who designed them.
- Start shopping. See the following sections for advice on where to go, what to wear, and whom and what to bring.
- Choose your dress. Remember that made-to-order gowns take a minimum of three to four months to be delivered to the bridal salon. Some couture gowns can take even longer. Even if you're buying off the rack or wearing a vintage gown, you'll need to reserve plenty of time for alterations.
- Prepare to make a 50 to 60 percent deposit, which should ideally be paid with a credit card.
- Before ordering, find out about your bridal shop's policies, including alteration fees, cancellation rules, and free services. Some salons offer package deal discounts on headpieces, veils, and other accessories with the purchase of a gown.

The Fine Art of Successful Shopping

- Get an estimated delivery date for your dress and find out when your balance is due.
- Get an idea of how many fittings will be required and how long the fitting process will take.
- You'll need a fabric swatch and use it to match your veil, shawl, shoes, and so on. Dye lots vary, so be sure to ask for a swatch of your actual dress fabric for a perfect match. The salon can send it to you after your dress is made.
- Professional wedding portraits are usually done well in advance of the event. Now is the time to book a prenup sitting with your photographer. If you're planning on a published announcement, you should know that many newspapers need to receive photos four to six weeks before the publication date. Adjust your schedule accordingly, and make sure your dress and headpiece will be ready in time for your photo session.
- Some salons will let you take your gown for photo sessions prior to your wedding. Then you can return it to the shop to be pressed so that it will be perfect for the wedding. Ask about your salon's policies regarding pressing dresses twice.
- Shop for and order your attendants' gowns.

Four to Six Months in Advance

- Select and order your headpiece and veil. If you're shopping at an upscale salon, you'll need a separate appointment.

- Call the salon to pinpoint your gown's delivery date.
- Shop for bridal undergarments, shoes, and accessories.

Two Months in Advance

- Schedule fitting appointments beginning about eight weeks before the wedding day.
- When your headpiece and veil are ready, begin your "hair trials"–that is, determine what kind of 'do you'll want for your wedding day.
- Audition various floral bouquet styles to see which best complements your look.

One Month to One Week in Advance

- Have your final fitting. Invite your maid of honor, mother, or whichever person is going to be securing your headpiece, fluffing your veil, carrying your train, and bustling your gown on the day of the wedding, so that she can have a trial run.
- Most brides pick up their gowns as close to the wedding day as possible, in order to avoid wrinkling or other mishaps.

TAKING CONTROL

In the early planning stages of your gown-shopping odyssey, you might be tempted to visit every single bridal emporium within a fifty-mile radius. This is not a good idea. Comparison shopping is essential, but brides who overshop run the risk of burning themselves out. Dresses all start looking the same . . . joy gives way to exhaustion or even resentment . . . and the inner compass that usually directs a woman's fashion sense ceases to do its job. Have you ever heard an exceptionally cranky bride-to-be announce that she never wants to see another white dress as long as she lives? That's a sure sign of wedding gown burnout.

Lara Westock remembers when she, with the help of her mother, began shopping for wedding gowns in January of 1999. "My mom called and said, 'I've been on the Internet for five hours, I've looked at fifty thousand gowns. Oh, my God.' She got married in 1967 when there were about three bridal stores," says Lara. "You went to one, you put your dress on, you bought it, that was it. Now you're bombarded with options."

Lara, who is now the bridal manager at Kleinfeld, believes that variety is both spicy and educational. But she also recognizes that too many choices can be overwhelming. "It can get to the point where it's too much. I fell in love with everything. It took me a year and a half to decide on a dress. It's like shopping for any big-ticket item: you're always going to find something nicer. You look at the Mercedes, the Jaguar's going to look even better. You look at an $8,000 dress, that $3,000 dress doesn't look so good anymore. If you find something that grabs you, stop right there."

Carole Romano, in her many years as a Kleinfeld bridal consultant, has counseled countless numbers of clients who have lost their bearings in a sea of options. "She has so much to do," Carole says of the modern fiancée. "The decision is all hers, and that pressure *is* overwhelming." To help soothe the stressed-out bride, Carole takes a gentle approach: "I sit her down in her private dressing room, make her comfortable, and talk to her." Though it doesn't take long for a bride to feel centered again, Carole knows that most of her clients are striving for perfection and try to accomplish too much in too little time.

So how many shops should you visit? The answer is three. Though you may think that number is about five stores shy of a real shopping expedition, stop for a moment and do the math: most bridal salons, even those that are on the small side or are tucked away on the top floor of a department store, offer a tremendous range of designer wedding gowns. (Space isn't much of an issue, because most keep only samples on hand.) Let's say you see ten dresses you like, try on eight of them, and one or two end up as possibilities. Repeat that scenario at two other stores offering different collections, and you can end up with three to six wonderful wedding dresses to choose from. How many more options would you really want?

Yes, you could argue that these seek-and-select figures are

arbitrary, and you'd be right. All three salon visits could easily result in zero possibilities, in which case you must expand your search.

On the other hand, if you're lucky enough to find The Dress at the first shop you visit, resist the urge to buy it right away. Go to other stores, take your time, and be sure that the gown you want is the gown you want. Three stores is not only the ideal maximum, it is also the ideal minimum.

PACING YOURSELF

Shopping takes a lot of energy. Unless you're terribly pressed for time, save yourself stress by scheduling only one appointment per shopping day. A single salon visit could take from one to three hours—not including travel time—and leave you with plenty to think about.

Bargain hunting in warehouses, outlets, or discount houses takes about ten times more effort than shopping in a salon. Prepare to roll up your sleeves and do battle—but please, limit your destinations to one or two large stores per day. Ultimately you'll get more done, and you'll greatly increase your odds of maintaining a cool head and a cheerful outlook.

WHERE WILL YOU FIND YOUR ONE TRUE DRESS?

The question of where to shop has much to do with economics. Full-service bridal salons are at the top of the food chain, so to speak, but they aren't the only game in town. Department stores, discount outlets, sample sales, vintage shops, and even consignment shops are good alternatives for brides who have more taste than money.

Bridal Salons

For women who love to shop, the high-end, Kleinfeld-style full-service bridal salon is a dream come true. There, in an elegant environment, you will be pampered, catered to, and given full license to try, test, critique, and covet some of the finest dresses in the world. Your wish is the bridal salon's command, whether your heart desires something simple, like a traditional-style gown that disguises your upper arms, or something challenging, like an avant-garde dress with a bodice edged in purple velvet. A salon is a place of almost endless possibilities, where adventurous brides can unleash their creativity and meticulous brides can get exactly what they want.

For women who hate to shop, the high-end, Kleinfeld-style full-service bridal salon is also a dream come true. There, brides can sit serenely in a private dressing room. Gowns that meet your requirements will be brought to you. You can try them on, ask questions, get advice, and never feel overwhelmed or pressured. Your headpiece, shoes, undergarments, and accessories can be quietly, privately previewed and purchased there as well.

At Kleinfeld gown prices start at about $1,800, with most styles falling in the $2,000–$5,000 range. Those dollars buy more than a dress, mind you: they also buy personal service that begins long before the sale and doesn't end until after you're safely married.

Virtually all bridal salons see clients on an "appointment only" basis. Try to schedule your appointment on a weekday, as evenings and weekends can become hectic in popular shops. When you call, you will probably be asked a series of basic questions regarding the date of your event and the general style of gown you're looking for. This is so your bridal consultant can get to know your needs in advance and serve you better when you arrive.

Department Stores

Certain department stores have their own full-service bridal salons. Though they may seem similar to independent or boutique bridal salons, alterations at major department stores are often handled at off-site facilities and performed by the same people who hem the pants on men's suits and take up the

Salon Samples

Most bridal salons have a certain number of samples available for sale at all times. Also known as "stock" dresses, these are gowns that have either been previously tried on by brides-to-be or are special orders that have been canceled. Though such gowns may not have the pristine cripness of a brand-new dress, they can be had for anywhere from 20 to 50 percent off the original retail price.

Kleinfeld bridal consultant Camille Coffey recalls one bride who ended up getting a $14,000 dress for $1,499. "It had been in the salon for a few years," says Camille, "but it was her dream dress, and it was the deal of the century."

A bride who buys a sample dress from a salon may go through the same fitting process as those who have their dresses custom made, with one possible added expense: she is usually responsible for the cleaning of the sample dress, which can be $100 or more, depending on where she lives.

sleeves on winter coats. On the plus side, department store salons sometimes offer less pricey house labels in addition to top-of-the-line designer pieces.

The Fine Art of Successful Shopping

Discount Bridal Shops

These mall-friendly shops generally stock popular styles in a whole range of sizes, just like regular mass-merchandise clothing stores. You can choose a dress and take it home that day or have basic alterations made as needed. A range of moderately priced bridal accessories is usually available, as are bridesmaids' ensembles.

Wedding Gown Outlets

Bridal outlet stores tend to be inelegant, strangely stocked, somewhat disorganized, and short on personal service. Past-season designer gowns might be jammed up against no-name brands in odd sizes. Pursue this option only if you're patient and don't mind digging for buried treasure. Note: At most outlet stores, you're on your own when it comes to alterations.

Sample Sales

Whether they're held by a store or hosted by a designer, these special sales are events in which samples—that is, gowns that have been tried on by future brides and/or models—are sold to the public at great savings. Sizes are usually limited to six, eight, and ten, but keep in mind that wedding dresses run

---

Big Ideas, Small Purse: Alternative Dress Sources

- Antique and vintage wedding gowns can be found at specialty shops, antiques shows (especially those dedicated to clothing and textiles), and all over the Internet.
- Consignment shops can be surprisingly fruitful: you might discover something fresh and unique, whether it's a couture creation from the 1960s or a spectacular custom gown made six months ago.
- Evening wear has been known to substitute for bridal wear. Have you looked at cocktail dresses, evening gowns, or even prom gowns? You might like what you see and save yourself serious money in the process.
- A talented seamstress is a treasure forever. You and a freelance dress-maker can come up with a design, choose just the right fabric, and make adjustments as you go along. Or you can pick out a pattern from a big book of wedding gown designs and add your own personal touches.
- Take a good look at the gown your mother wore. Then raid your aunties' attics. Though at first glance they might seem hopelessly corny, gowns from bygone eras can be cut down, revamped, and reborn as contemporary masterpieces . . . as long as the gown has been well preserved and the fabric is in perfect or near perfect condition.

---

small and that some salons feature a broader range of sample sizes. Sample gowns are rarely in perfect shape. If you're willing to spend a little extra to repair minor blemishes—strained seams, tiny rips, traces of makeup here and there—the right sample gown can be the bargain of the century.

The Fine Art of Successful Shopping

SHOPPING FOR SHOPS

Your time is precious—especially now, when your whole life seems to hinge on a series of increasingly urgent deadlines. You'll save yourself hours and days by planning your shopping trips carefully and targeting only the stores that have good reputations and offer the styles you're looking for. Some strategies:

- If a certain designer's work has caught your eye, chances are you can find his or her contact number in magazine ads or in the resources section that follows editorial fashion layouts. Most design houses have a toll-free number that will lead you to stores in your area that are authorized dealers of their merchandise.
- Look up your favorite designers on the Internet; many Web sites include lists of authorized dealers.
- Word of mouth is powerful. Seek out recommendations and advice from as many real brides as you can. You might be directed to an excellent salon and the name of a stellar bridal consultant.

ALL THE RIGHT QUESTIONS

Is your short list of shops in place? Good. Now, before you schedule actual appointments, call each one of them and conduct a short interview of your own. You'll want to ask:

How to Buy Your Perfect Wedding Dress

Maximum Glamour:
Designer Trunk Shows

Top bridal salons offer an assortment of gowns by world-class wedding designers. But no salon can stock every gown in every designer's line— even Kleinfeld, which has the largest selection in the country. Therefore, design houses regularly present "trunk shows" at leading salons, during which their entire line is displayed and made available to brides. For women who seek rare, avant-garde, or even one-of-a-kind styles, the trunk show is a fabulous opportunity to achieve maximum glamour.

- How many different gown styles are represented? (There is no wrong answer to this question, but it will give you an idea of the relative size of the salon.)
- What is the average gown price?
- Will a bridal consultant be assigned to me, or will I be on my own?
- Will my consultant give me access to all the gowns, or will she select samples for me?
- What gown sizes are available to try on? (Remember that wedding gown sizes run about two sizes smaller than regular women's wear.)
- How long does it usually take for a gown to be delivered?
- Are fittings and alterations taken care of by the salon? Are they done on the premises? What is the price policy for fit-

tings and alterations? Are any fitting sessions included in the price of the gown?

- How much time should be allowed between the initial dress order and the final fitting? (If you're in a hurry, ask about rush services and get the details on applicable surcharges.)
- Does the shop sell headpieces, veils, shoes, lingerie, accessories? If so, are these items discounted for those brides who buy their gowns at the shop?
- Is there a selection of bridesmaids' dresses on-site? Is there a package deal for the bride and her bridal party?
- What is the standard payment schedule? Does the salon issue a contract upon deposit? Is the deposit refundable? At what point is the balance due? What recourse does the client have if the dress isn't delivered on time, doesn't meet expectations, or breaches the contract in any way?

YOUR SHOPPING COMPANION, AND HOW TO CHOOSE HER

Batman has Robin. Xena has Gabrielle. Barbie has Skipper. And you, the bride-to-be who has been called upon to accomplish incredible feats of fashion within a small window of time, deserve an able sidekick who will complement your shopping powers perfectly. Before lining up your candidates, learn these basic ground rules:

How to Buy Your Perfect Wedding Dress

Silent Second Opinions

One of Kleinfeld bridal consultant Renée Pinto's brides had decided on a contemporary beaded sheath that she and her best friend both adored. Before making the purchase, the bride brought her mom in for final approval. Mom loved it but asked her daughter to try on one poufy dress as a special favor. "She put on a princess gown with a big tulle skirt," says Renée. The mother burst into tears but didn't say a word. "There was no pressure, no pushing," reports Renée. Entirely on her own, the bride passed on the sophisticated sheath and chose the dress with the poufy skirt. The moral of the story: Second opinions, even when they're unspoken, can speak volumes.

- Shop with only one or two people at a time. Too many opinions are counterproductive.
- Bring the same person with you on inaugural visits to your chosen salons or shops. You'll want to share first impressions with a trusted friend who knows what you know.
- Bring a different person with you when you're visiting salons or shops for the second time. A second opinion couldn't hurt.
- Don't bring your children or anyone else's children. This is your opportunity to be the center of the universe.

So . . . who are the chosen few who will shop with you? First, make a list of your top nominees, including your mother, your sisters, your maid of honor, your bridesmaids, your childhood best friend, your future female in-laws, and your neighbor who has impeccable taste and once worked for Martha Stewart. Put sentiment aside for a moment and ruthlessly rate each potential shopping companion according to the following quiz:

1. Do you like her style?
   a. Not really; many of her fashion and decorating choices are not to my taste.
   b. Sure. She puts things together in an attractive, pleasing way.
   c. Definitely; I'm impressed by her artistic touch and her originality.

2. Is she honest with you?
   a. Not entirely. She tends to keep her opinions to herself.
   b. Sure. When she feels strongly about something, she makes her feelings known.
   c. Yes, but her judgment calls can be harsh and aren't always welcome.

3. Do you respect her opinions?
   a. Sometimes, but her opinions often seem like platitudes.
   b. Yes. Though I don't always agree with her, she usually forms thoughtful opinions before speaking out.
   c. Sometimes. She can be brilliant and inspiring, but she can also be impulsive, impractical, and/or controlling.

4. Is she sensitive to your needs—including your requirements, restrictions, and limitations?
   a. Yes, to the extent that she'll emphasize practical issues and devalue what is whimsical or extravagant.
   b. Yes. She's the voice of reason, but she doesn't discourage me from taking calculated risks.
   c. Not particularly. She tends to enforce her agenda, even if it's impractical for me.

5. Is she fun to shop with?
   a. Maybe not, but she'll get me to my appointments on time and ask tough questions about contracts, costs, schedules, and more.
   b. Yes. She's upbeat and tuned in to what I want and what I need.
   c. Yes, but she has a tendency to be pushy and might try to direct me toward styles that she loves and I don't.

Scoring

Three or more "a" answers: This potential shopping pal is stodgy and plodding. Is it your mother? Your grandmother? Your great-aunt? Never mind: she may be dull, but if you're the type who is seduced by every pretty gown that comes down the pike, you probably need a party pooper in your dressing room. Take her along on your first round of gown shopping.

The Mother Question

Renata Valle, a Kleinfeld bridal consultant, still cringes when she remembers the mother of a bride who turned to her daughter and said, "You're going to wear that gown, like it or not."

When Kleinfeld consultant Rosaria Schiano has to deal with an overbearing mother, she diffuses the situation with humor. "I turn to the bride and say, 'When you have a daughter, you can have your own wedding, but right now this is Mom's special day.' "

Though both consultants have horror stories, both agree that most moms who shop with their daughters are gentle, loving, and respectful. "They relish the bonding experience so much that they don't want it to end," says Rosaria. "They'll try to extend the process; they caution their daughters against picking out the gown too quickly." As for Renata, she estimates that 80 percent of the mothers she interacts with are highly sensitive to their daughters' feelings. "Most are too shy to express themselves," says Renata. "They'll say, 'Which dress do you like better?' They're wonderful, supportive. They rarely impose their opinions."

Where does your mom fit in? Even if she's a candidate for sainthood, many brides-to-be are uncomfortable shopping with their mothers but feel obligated to include them in the process. It's a difficult situation, especially if Mom is helping to pay for the dress. But even if she isn't, the average mother places a tremendous sentimental value on the act of going shopping for her daughter's wedding gown. The daughter who will not shop with her mother runs the risk of offending or even wounding her *mother. Which is not only unkind but unwise, since it can cause tension that may resonate well beyond the wedding day. But what of the bride whose mother is controlling and manipulative and is apt to railroad her poor daughter into buying the wrong gown?*

A newlywed of our acquaintance solved this dilemma in a brilliant way: she did three months of heavy-duty shopping with her best friend. Then, when it came down to choosing among the top three gown finalists, she invited her mother along to help pick the winner. Our bride loved all three, so she knew she would be happy no matter what. Mom was delighted to be included and felt a warm sense of belonging . . . not to mention a satisfying soupçon of power.

Three or more "b" answers: Ahh. A true friend. She'll keep you on course but won't hold you back; she'll tell you which gowns make you look stunning and which ones make you look so-so; and, if the dress is right, she'll help you figure out how to squeeze another $500 out of your budget to pay for it. If you're lucky enough to have such a friend in your life, take her with you any time major bridal decisions need to be made.

Three or more "c" answers: This fearless female is the one to take along if you're insecure about your choices or feel intimidated by the salon environment. She'll run the whole show if you let her. Invite this friend on one of your rounds, but make sure to counteract her influence: don't buy anything until you've also consulted an "a" or "b" shopper.

The Fine Art of Successful Shopping

WHAT TO BRING

Now that you know where you're going and whom you're bringing, it's time to pack a small bag with shopping essentials.

Top Twelve Items to Bring on a Wedding Gown Shopping Trip

1. Photos of four or five gowns you love, gleaned from magazines and Web pages.

2. A list or an idea of what you want and need in a wedding gown, including your ideal color, the level of formality you seek, and which of your physical features you'd like to play up or disguise.

3. Brideworthy (white) underwear, including a strapless bra (with padded cups, if you'll be needing them), and control-top panty hose (or a similar body-slimming undergarment).

4. Shoes with the same height of heel that you'd like to wear on your wedding day.

5. The veil or headpiece you plan to wear—if, for example, you will be wearing your grandmother's headpiece, bring it along on every trip.

6. Grooming aids, including a hairbrush, scrunchies, or clips, so you can put your hair up if needed. Avoid wearing excessive makeup, lipstick, and jewelry because they can damage a dress.

7. Contact lenses (instead of glasses), if that's what you'll be wearing on your wedding day.

8. Reading glasses, if you need them to make out the fine print on contracts.

9. A camera, if your bridal salon allows them.

10. A bottle of water or other nonstaining beverage (no coffee or red wine, please!).

11. The following shopping log and a pen.

12. Tissues.

Where I've Been and What I've Tried On:
A Bride's Shopping Log

Store name: _____

Address: _____

Phone/fax/e-mail/Web site: _____

Consultant/contact person: _____

Date visited: _____

Potential gown no. 1:

Description _____

Color_____Fabric_____

Designer_____Size_____

Style no. (if available) _____

Price_____ Alterations charge_____

Estimated delivery time _____

Pros_____

Cons_____

Notes_____

_____

Potential gown no. 2:

Description _____

_____

Color _____

Fabric _____

Designer _____

Style no. (if available) _____

Size _____

Price _____

Alterations charge _____

Estimated delivery time _____

Pros _____

Cons _____

Notes _____

_____

_____

_____

Potential gown no. 3:

Description _____

_____

Color _____

Fabric _____

Designer _____

Style no. (if available) _____

Size _____

Price _____

Alterations charge _____

Estimated delivery time _____

Pros _____

Cons _____

Notes _____

_____

_____

_____

Store name: _____

Address: _____

Phone/fax/e-mail/Web site: _____

Consultant/contact person: _____

Date visited: _____

Potential gown no. 4:

Description _____

Color_____ Fabric_____

Designer_____ Size_____

Style no. (if available) _____

Price_____ Alterations charge_____

Estimated delivery time _____

Pros_____

Cons_____

Notes_____

_____

_____

Potential gown no. 5:

Description _____

_____

Color _____

Fabric _____

Designer _____

Style no. (if available) _____

Size _____

Price _____

Alterations charge _____

Estimated delivery time _____

Pros _____

Cons _____

Notes _____

_____

_____

_____

Potential gown no. 6:

Description _____

_____

Color _____

Fabric _____

Designer _____

Style no. (if available) _____

Size _____

Price _____

Alterations charge _____

Estimated delivery time _____

Pros _____

Cons _____

Notes _____

_____

_____

_____

Store name: _____

Address: _____

Phone/fax/e-mail/Web site: _____

Consultant/contact person: _____

Date visited: _____

Potential gown no. 7:

Description _____

Color_____ Fabric_____

Designer_____ Size_____

Style no. (if available) _____

Price_____ Alterations charge_____

Estimated delivery time _____

Pros _____

Cons_____

Notes_____

_____

_____

Potential gown no. 8:

Description _____

_____

Color _____

Fabric _____

Designer _____

Style no. (if available) _____

Size _____

Price _____

Alterations charge _____

Estimated delivery time _____

Pros _____

Cons _____

Notes _____

_____

_____

_____

Potential gown no. 9:

Description _____

_____

Color _____

Fabric _____

Designer _____

Style no. (if available) _____

Size _____

Price _____

Alterations charge _____

Estimated delivery time _____

Pros _____

Cons _____

Notes _____

_____

_____

_____

SECRETS OF THE DRESSING ROOM, PART 1: DON'T DARE TO BE BARE

Have you ever been to a fashion photo shoot or hung around backstage at a runway show? If so, you'll have noticed that models prance around half-naked without an ounce of modesty. They're totally accustomed to whipping off their clothes and relaxing in tiny panties, a skimpy bra, or nothing at all.

Do not attempt this level of casual nudity at a bridal salon. Even though dressing rooms at high-end salons are private, the bride does share the room with her consultant—who has to be there to help her in and out of dresses—and her shopping companions. "Some brides come with no underwear at all," says Kleinfeld bridal consultant Dyan Bonjourno. "They're nude in my room. So it's me, their butt, and the zipper." She's worked with brides-to-be who invite their entire families along—and have nothing but a thong underneath their clothes. "Hello!" says Dyan with a good-natured laugh. "They just don't realize how exposed they're going to be."

Professional consultants recommend that brides wear "decent" underwear, panty hose, and a long-line bra, preferably strapless and backless. (Kleinfeld provides such bras as a service to their clients, but brides with less accommodating salons should consider purchasing one before shopping.)

If modesty forbids you from being seen in your underwear by anyone, including your mother, your best friend, and your consultant, then you should buy yourself a full slip before you set foot in a bridal salon. We're talking about a long slip that covers your bust, waist, hips, thighs, knees, and whatever else you want to keep under wraps. Though strapless slips are best, they can be hard to come by, so just look for a slim-fitting, preferably stretchy number in white, off-white, or whatever shade of nude best matches your skin tone.

With the proper undergarments, you will spare yourself the humiliation of having a virtual stranger wrestle hooks and zippers around your bare flesh. And that stoic handmaiden—your bridal consultant—will thank you for it.

Are You Ready for Your Close-Up? A Cautionary Tale

Kleinfeld bridal consultant Rita Dato remembers a dressing room gaffe that almost ruined an entire wedding. "One of my brides brought her big Italian family to the salon," recalls Rita, "including Grandma, who was paying for the dress." When the bride stripped down in the dressing room to try on the gown, her female relatives got an eyeful: the name Tony was tattooed in large letters across the small of her back. The grandmother was horrified to learn that her precious granddaughter had gotten a tattoo that she threatened to boycott the whole wedding. Emotions heated to the boiling point. "The family eventually worked it out," reports Rita, but only after hours of tearful negotiations.

The moral of the story should be familiar to any bride who was ever a Girl Scout: be prepared.

Dream a Little Dream

Albertina Simone never imagined she'd be shopping for her wedding dress all by herself. "I moved to New York City from Michigan in July 1999," she explains. "My boyfriend and I became engaged that November." Though her future husband was a Brooklyn native, "My mom wasn't there, my sister wasn't there, and my maid of honor wasn't there," she says.

Albertina found her way to Kleinfeld, and from that moment on she didn't feel alone. "The sales people were fantastic," she says. "They would gently make comments, they took very good personal care of me. I didn't feel like just another bride."

Margaret LoGiudice guided Albertina to a silk organza gown, designed by Candice Solomon, that suited her perfectly and was formal enough for her ceremony at St. Patrick's Cathedral in Manhattan. "It was strapless, with a fitted top that was detailed with pearls and crystals," she says. The back of the dress featured a row of covered buttons and a collection of silk roses at the dropped waistline, which led to a dramatically wide skirt. "We had a rose theme to our wedding—there were roses on the invitations, and our reception was at the Rose Room at the Plaza Hotel." Albertina's only concern was that she wanted a very long veil—at least five yards—that would drape down the steps when she stood at the main altar."

Albertina ordered the dress. Then, over the Christmas holidays, her subconscious began to stir. "I woke up from a vivid dream one night," she says. "The dream told me that there was a dress at Bergdorf's that I should have bought." At 11:30 that night, Albertina left a message for Ronnie at Kleinfeld. He called her back first thing in the morning. "I told him about my dream and asked if I could see him the next day. I thought maybe Kleinfeld carried the same dress and we could work something out. He said, 'If you really want that other gown, I'll call the designer personally and see if we can cancel production of the gown.' " Albertina was so touched, she decided then and there to keep doing business with Kleinfeld. "It was my sign that I had already chosen the right dress," she says.

Albertina Simone married Sal Mario Varano on May 20, 2000. "I hadn't told my fiancé one thing about the dress," she says. "When I walked down the aisle, the organ music filled the cathedral, my dress was swirling around me, and I felt as if I were levitating. The emotions were overwhelming. When I reached him, he was misty-eyed, with a huge smile on his face. He told me I looked like a white cloud floating down the aisle."

Albertina and Sal live in Michigan now, but Albertina's wedding gown experience is never far from her mind. "When I think about my wedding day, which is by far the best day of my life, Kleinfeld is always part of the memory. It's a happy place for me to go back to."

Chapter Four

The Day of the Dress

READY . . .

Be excited. Go tanning if you're going to be tan; put your hair up if it's going to be up; get a good night's sleep; be in love; wear conservative makeup that won't rub off on white silk; drink plenty of water; eat a decent breakfast; pack the top twelve items listed in chapter 3; wear an outfit that's easy to slip on and off; call in advance to see if the salon's appointments are running on schedule. Be a bride.

SET . . .

While you prepare yourself physically, look inside yourself and contemplate the ancient wisdom of yin and yang. Notice these dichotomies:

- You, the bride, are expected to be both blushing and businesslike.
- You're about to purchase the most feminine—and fabulous—dress of your life . . . even while you're carrying a bulging date book and barking out orders to caterers, florists, hoteliers, and others.
- You're pleased that your mother has offered to pay for the dress . . . but you dread her actual input or opinions.
- Your heart is set on white. You hope that your priest/minister/rabbi/father doesn't ask any questions.
- You feel slightly squeamish about the cost of the dress . . . but you're sure that the purchase will stimulate the local economy and create lasting memories for your loved ones and future generations . . . right?
- You want a nontraditional wedding . . . yet you forbid your groom to see your gown before the ceremony, insisting that it's bad luck.

Yin vs. yang, dark vs. light, old vs. new, customary vs. custom-made: welcome to the precarious balancing act of the modern bride. Please don't feel guilty, ashamed, or crazy: it's all good, totally normal and healthy. The key to your inner peace is to embrace the contradictions. Every wedding is a seesaw, in which the bride's will is pitched against the expectations of others. Ultimately, it is that surprising counterbalance of concessions and assertions that paves the way for a perfect wedding day.

Yin and yang. That's you.

SHOP!

Your first day out might be a swirl of gorgeous gowns and visions of loveliness, but shopping gets serious when it comes time to make decisions. So in keeping with the laws of yin and yang, it's imperative that you—or better yet, your shopping companion—take copious notes throughout the process. Keep track of all the dresses, even the ones that don't work, in both words and pictures. Make notations about your consultant, the shop, its selection, and its vibes. Don't fool yourself into thinking that you'll be able to keep these details in your head. You won't.

In order to keep plenty of fun in the shopping formula, be sure to pace yourself. Though you might be tempted to plow through the shop's selection with the tenacity of a pit bull, it's much more pleasant (and productive) to take your sweet time. Be sensitive to the energy and patience levels of yourself and your shopping partner. Relax. Breathe. If you start to feel overwhelmed or stressed, take a break and walk around the block. When your enthusiasm finally droops, call it a day. Don't worry if there are still five or six dresses you'd like to see yourself in. You can, and will, come back for more.

When the day is done, go treat your shopping pal to lunch or supper in a restaurant where you can pore over your notes and pictures and digest all the information you've gathered. The après-shopping meal should be a time for jubilance.

The Day of the Dress

SECRETS OF THE DRESSING ROOM, PART 2: CLOSED STOCK

Many high-end bridal salons have what's known as "closed stock." This means that although you can view those gowns on display in the showroom, you can't see every available style or sample because of the way in which the gowns are stored. Rather, once you've bonded with your consultant, you're ensconced in your own private dressing room, where appropriate samples are brought for your approval. The closed-stock system is designed to make shopping more efficient. Considering that the largest salons may have hundreds of different gowns in stock, it saves an enormous amount of time when an enlightened consultant presorts your options for you.

"Closed stock is the only way to go," says Kleinfeld bridal consultant Vivian Solmo. She points out that the majority of gown samples are placed in plastic bags for the gowns' protection and hung together. "There's no way that a bride can see what a dress on a hanger in a plastic garment bag really looks like." But Vivian softens her stance for experienced brides. "If a girl has been to four or five salons and really knows what she's looking for, I'll say, 'Would you like to come and shop with me?' "

Though the closed-stock system may take a bit of getting used to, it helps to think of your bridal consultant as a wine steward or sommelier in a fine restaurant. He or she is intimately familiar with the hundreds of wines in the restaurant's cellar. Though you could plow through a twelve-page wine list and make an educated guess, it makes much more sense to tell a sommelier what you're having for dinner, how much you'd like to spend, and any personal preferences you might have. Chances are he or she will select the perfect list for you to choose from.

MAKING THE MOST OF YOUR BRIDAL CONSULTANT

The best salon relationships are those built on trust. Your bridal consultant is a professional; she's seen an enormous number of brides in all shapes and sizes. With her educated eye, she can assess your body in a matter of minutes and know which gown styles will flatter your figure. But it's up to you to guide her down your personal style path.

"Shopping is like a maze," says Dorothy Silver, director of merchandising and sales, who has been mentoring brides-to-be at Kleinfeld for twelve years. "My ideal client is a bride who has done her homework, because the more information she gives me, the faster I can find her dress. We have over one thousand gowns here; I need directional signals."

Dorothy has a basic path she follows when hunting for the perfect dress. "The first thing we do is decide on a shape," she says. "Fitted with a full skirt? Okay. Now, what do we want going on around the shoulders and arms? Strapless? Great.

The Day of the Dress

What about decoration? Beading? Fabulous! Off I go. And I can get all the beaded, strapless, fitted-with-a-full-skirt gowns that might work for her."

Dorothy also appreciates a bride who has opinions and isn't afraid to express them. "Some girls know themselves," she says. "They can say, 'I don't like this dress,' or, 'I like this shape but not this trim right here.'" Her job is much easier when a bride tells it like it is; her toughest customers are those who stand at the mirror and say, "I don't know," or, "I'm waiting for it to hit me." Dorothy does her best to coax them. "I tell the brides, 'Look, I didn't design this dress, you're not going to hurt my feelings.'"

Honesty is important, explains Kleinfeld bridal consultant Debbie Lakis, because once a consultant zeroes in on a style of gown that pleases the bride, it's the details that make all the difference. "At that point, I learn more from knowing what a bride doesn't like," she says. "Once you get those components together—what she wants versus what she doesn't want—there's the dress."

TRY IT, YOU MIGHT LIKE IT

Good bridal consultants tend to build relationships with their clients. It's only natural: as Lucille Inglese, a bridal consultant at Kleinfeld, points out, "This is the only business in the world where you spend nine to twelve or more months with the customer. It's personal." So once in a while, a bridal consultant might ask you to try on a gown that doesn't seem to meet your criteria or taste. Indulge her, okay? She probably knows something that you don't . . . and many a bride has floated down the aisle in a gown that she never thought she could or would wear. Whatever your final choice, be assured that between the consultant's experience and your taste, the two of you can cut through a jungle of wedding gowns and find a precious jewel.

HOW DO YOU KNOW WHEN YOU'VE FOUND THE ONE?

What a scary decision. This gown is going to be the centerpiece of your wedding, the ultimate expression of your personal style, and it will be scrutinized and photographed by every person you love. It's a big investment on many levels. And like most major investments, it's a commitment that isn't easy to back out of. For many brides, saying "I do" to the dress is more difficult than saying "I do" to the man they're marrying.

So how do you know when you've found the best dress in the whole universe? You might try taking a vote, but experts say that doesn't help. "I've had brides come in with their whole bridal party—six girlfriends, mother, aunt, cousins—and it never works out," reports bridal consultant Toni Ann Galati. "Because if the bride likes something, at least one person is going to object. There are too many opinions."

The Day of the Dress

"It's Not You, It's the Gown": How to Break Up with Your Bridal Consultant

Uh-oh. You've bonded with two (or more) consultants at competing salons. You love them both—really!—but you like one dress better than the other and the time has come for you to choose a dress. And one (or more) of your beloved bridal consultants is going to take a fall.

Technically, you're not obligated to buy a dress at any salon, no matter how many times you've visited or how many hours you've spent with a consultant (assuming you haven't signed a contract, of course). But brides and their consultants tend to form strong bonds that transcend legal gibberish and contractual twaddle. You've told this woman your hopes, your dreams, your fears, your fashion phobias. She's seen you in your underwear and has perhaps even negotiated peace treaties between you and your mother. So how are you going to tell her that you 1) have been cheating on her; and 2) are going to sign on someone else's dotted line?

As with all emotional unpleasantries, breaking up with your consultant requires maturity and compassion. The wrong way to do it is to just disappear into the mist without so much as an explanation, much less a thank-you. The right way is to summon up your courage, pick up the phone, and tell the truth.

Bridal manager Lara Westock recalls the sad day that one of "her" brides, a three-time visitor, broke the news: "She loved a dress here and loved a different dress at another salon," says Lara. "She called me, she was very sweet, and said, 'I'm really sorry, but the other dress just turned out to be it.' And

I said, 'I just want you to be happy.'" Lara admits that such incidents can be frustrating. "The salesperson part of me was like, 'Arrgh!' But the person-person part of me understood. The last thing I wanted was for her to walk down the aisle in something she didn't love."

So be civil. If you've developed a relationship with a bridal consult-ant but decide on buying your dress elsewhere, the kind and decent thing to do is to make a call and let her down gently. After all, you might end up changing your mind . . . again.

Lara Westock, who is not only the Kleinfeld bridal manager but also a Kleinfeld bride, has seen clients get bogged down by practical considerations. "They say, 'Can I wear it again? Can I dye it black and wear it to a cocktail party?' Personally, I think it should be a once-in-a-lifetime experience. The gown should be amazing, a fairy-tale thing." Lara has noticed that when a future bride stops trying to make her dress earn its keep, she's free to please herself and fulfill her fantasies. "I could wear a slinky dress anywhere," notes Lara. "I think a wedding gown should be something you couldn't, and wouldn't, wear again."

In her twelve years at Kleinfeld, Dorothy Silver has seen many clients who would look at nothing but chic, minimalist sheaths. But sometimes one of these thoroughly modern brides would emerge from the dressing room and have a change of heart. "Next to her, in the mirror, is another bride who's wearing a fantasy dress with all the embellishments—a fairy-tale gown," says Dorothy. "Many brides are professional women; a lot of them worry about wearing full dresses. But it can turn around completely. All of a sudden they want the Cinderella look. We had a bride who was fifty years old who went the whole nine yards—big wedding gown, dramatic headpiece."

Though the road to cloud nine might be unpredictable, Roseann Clerkin believes that it leads to an indisputable moment of truth. "When it's the bride's gown, it's the bride's gown," says Roseann. "She knows when she puts it on that it's the magic dress."

According to bridal consultant Vasiliki Livathinos, the bride's expression says it all. "The face tells me everything," says Vasiliki. "When the gown is right, she doesn't want to take it off. Mom starts crying. I run and get a veil and headpiece and walk them out to that big mirror. We're all on the same page. It's my favorite part of the job—to see the bride walk out of here on a cloud."

ORDERING YOUR DRESS

If you've been faithfully filling out the bride's shopping log in chapter 3, then most of your crucial questions have already been answered.

Now it's time to get down to nitty-gritty details:

How to Buy Your Perfect Wedding Dress

- Be measured for the dress. Your measurements will determine your gown size, depending on the manufacturer's specifications. Remember that wedding gown sizes run small, so your gown will probably be ordered at least two sizes larger than what you usually wear. Don't fret. Keep in mind that during the fitting process, it's easier and more efficient to take seams in and hems up than it is to let seams out and hems down.
- Make decisions about alterations. Work closely with your consultant on these points; you want to make sure that what you have in mind won't be a problem for the fittings department.
- Agree on alterations fees and a general fittings schedule.
- Find out if the purchase of the dress qualifies you for discounts on accessories, bridesmaids' dresses, and so forth.
- Find out if you can have the dress in advance of the scheduled pickup date if you're planning on sitting for a prewedding portrait.

A FITTING JOB

The fitting of your dress is an intricate and expert affair—and takes more time than you might think. "The average gown requires at least twenty-two hours to alter," says Nitsa Glezelis, Kleinfeld's director of alterations. "With every adjustment the artisans have to take the whole gown apart, then put it back together perfectly. That means matching beading, lace, edging,

The Day of the Dress

everything." Once the handiwork is done, the dress has to be prepped and pressed—and hand-pressing alone can easily take three hours.

Special alterations—custom embroidering a bodice, for example, or adapting the neckline or sleeves of a dress—usually require additional charges. Penny Touranont, manager of Kleinfeld's beading department, has created special-order bridal embellishments for nearly twenty years. Her department turns out masterpieces, but there is no cutting corners when it comes to hand-sewing crystals or executing fine embroidery. Penny recalls a particular job in which she adapted a decorative motif from a gown and reproduced it, in beads, on a twenty-five-foot train. "It took months," she says.

If you want to add custom decorations to your dress or make significant changes to its original design, it's important that you have a serious conference with your consultant (and the head of the fittings department, if possible).

"Most alterations are about taking things off, not putting things on," says Kleinfeld bridal consultant Debbie Asprea. Brides are usually confident about removing such details as flowers, bows, and beads. But when it comes to adding design elements, bravery fades away. "It can be hard to visualize add-ons," says Debbie. "Most girls are afraid to buy something they can't see."

Add-ons can be expensive as well. Among Kleinfeld's clients are brides who, because of religious requirements, need to add long sleeves and high necklines to whatever gown they choose. Such alterations are known as "build-ups" and can add $700 or more to the cost of a dress. There are less elaborate build-ups, of course—such as adding a panel of illusion lace to a backless gown—and each is priced according to its complexity.

Before you order a dress with alterations, make sure that your ideas are understood and accepted; you're given either an estimate with a ceiling price or a flat fee for the custom work, and a projected schedule that you feel comfortable with.

PAYING FOR YOUR DRESS

When you are finally ready to commit to a gown and are prepared to put down your 50 or 60 percent deposit, you'll be asked to sign a contract. Read it carefully and make sure that the following points are covered:

- Designer's or manufacturer's identification
- Style number
- Color ordered
- Size ordered
- Price quoted
- Fittings estimate (cost and what it covers)
- Special alterations ordered
- Other costs (pressing, shipping, and so on)
- Estimated date the dress will be delivered to store

The Day of the Dress

Your Partner, Your Salon

Let's say you've found two wonderful gowns at two different salons and simply can't make up your mind. Here's a tip: After agonizing about the cut, fabric, and price of the gowns, set your sights on choosing the better bridal shop. This is an important consideration: after all, you will be in partnership with the salon of your choice for six months or more. You will be visiting the salon again and again and will be depending on the salon's management, suppliers, shippers, artisans, and fitters—not to mention your bridal consultant—to get every detail right and to meet a series of serious deadlines.

When rating a bridal salon, take note of the following:

- Were you welcomed promptly and given immediate attention? Different salons have different procedures, but a client should always be acknowledged in a personal, hospitable way the minute she walks through the door, whether it's her first or her tenth time there.)

- Were you made to wait more than fifteen minutes before being interviewed or meeting with your sales consultant? (Running a salon is an art, not a science, and sometimes appointments are delayed a bit. If this is the case, the greeter or receptionist should immediately give you, the client, an estimated waiting time, so you have the option of scoping out the neighborhood, getting coffee, or running an errand instead of sitting in nervous anticipation.)

- When being interviewed by your consultant, did you feel that you were asked relevant questions and allowed to give your truest answers? Conversely, did you feel as if you were being squeezed into cookie-cutter

> categories that didn't make room for your unique opinions, quirks, and concerns?
> - Were you pleased with your personal consultant and her efforts? Did she respect your vision, understand your fashion sense, and go the extra mile to find gowns that suited your style, flattered your body, and fell within your price range? Was she honest? Was she patient?
> - Did you feel rushed or pressured to leave a deposit on a dress you weren't sure of?
> - Did you like the salon's selections?
> - Were you informed of prices, designers, estimated delivery times, and policies?
> - Were you treated warmly on your way out and given an opportunity to air your concerns, ask questions, and/or make additional appointments?
> - On follow-up visits, were you welcomed like an old friend? Did you pick up where you left off with your usual sales consultant, or were you handed off to a new one?

- Date the dress must be ready for pickup
- Deposit amount required and paid
- Future payments schedule and date balance is due
- Cancellation/refunds policy
- General terms of sale

Finally, note that many salons will ask for an authorization signature so that they can automatically charge your unpaid balance to your credit card on the day that your dress arrives at the store. If you want to use a different card to pay your balance, now is the time to speak up.

The Day of the Dress

Who Will Pay?

Traditionally, the bride's family pays for her dress. But that custom is by no means universal. In Egypt, for instance, the groom and his family foot the bill for bridal wear—and that cost can be substantial, since well-to-do Egyptian brides often wear wedding gowns embellished with real jewels.

Cultural customs aside, the question of who pays for the dress is increasingly open to interpretation, even in old-fashioned American families. "Today, it's a whole different bride," explains director of merchandising and sales Dorothy Silver. "Ten years ago, the bride would come with Mom, Dad, Grandma. Today, we see lots of first-time brides who are working women; they're paying for their weddings, they're buying their own dresses. Many of the brides are coming alone and buying alone. They have great confidence and style."

Bridal consultant Judith Lerner is well aware of the trend. "It's not like the old days when the bride's family automatically bought the gown," she notes. "The parents might come, but the bride pulls out the credit card." Judith has also seen generous grandparents make the gown their wedding gift and has worked with at least one groom who helped choose the gown and picked up the tab, too.

The bottom line is that today's brides are rewriting the rules. A wedding gown might indeed be paid for by a bride's parents, but it's not unusual for it to be bought by a sibling, an elder relative, a group of friends, the in-laws, or the bride herself.

Chapter Five

All About Accessories

Your wedding gown makes a sweeping statement about your style, your ceremony, and your future life with the man you love. But the picture isn't complete until you choose your bridal accessories, and it is these details—veil, headpiece, wrap, gloves, jewelry, shoes—that make you shine like the star you are.

IT'S A WRAP: THE COVER STORY

Cover-ups are sort of the orphan children of bridal wear. Though a few designers offer wedding capes and coats, the bride who wants to drape her shoulders, warm her neck, or cloak herself head to toe against winter winds is often left to her own creative devices. No need to despair: appropriate cover-ups can be found in all sorts of retail environments, including department stores, furriers' salons, evening wear boutiques, and, yes, bridal emporiums. It's not unusual for a high-end salon to create custom wraps for brides. According to

Nitsa Glezelis, director of alterations at Kleinfeld, her department routinely turns out boleros, jackets, shawls, capes, and more. "We can make a pattern according to a bride's wishes," says Nitsa, "and create the garment in fabrics that coordinate with her ensemble."

You can protect yourself from chills and other unfriendly forces with any one of the following pieces:

Bolero: A long-sleeved jacket with a short body that ends just below the bustline. Traditionally worn by Spanish bullfighters, authentic boleros are stiffly structured and adorned with jewels and embroidery.

Shrug: Not quite a jacket, the shrug is composed of two long sleeves that meet at the back, with little or no fabric showing at the front of the bodice.

Stole: Also known as a "wrap," this long, rectangular piece of fabric is meant to be thrown about the shoulders and taken off at will. A favorite stole for cool weather is the pashmina, made of luxuriously soft cashmere from the Himalayas. Stoles can be jeweled or embroidered, backed with contrasting fabric, trimmed with fringe or fur, or made entirely of fur.

Jacket: Depending on your dress, an appropriate cover-up might be a tuxedo jacket, a blazer, or a peplum-style jacket that flares at the waist. Or how about a short jacket with furry, fuzzy, or feathery trim?

Coat: Once in a while, a couture designer offers a sumptuous bridal coat that complements wedding gowns sublimely. If you can't get your hands on such a coat, but weather conditions require that you wear one, you might consider having a coat custom-made.

Cape: An armless cloak, with or without a hood. Capes can be as long as the train on your wedding dress or fall just shy of floor length. The warmest capes are lined with fur or faux fur, which might also appeal to a bride's inner princess.

Capelet: A short version of the cape. Some capelets are so small that they're little more than a glorified collar; they still add warmth, however, especially to strapless gowns.

One-sleeved shawl: New to the bridal market, this elegant wrap features one sleeve. The bride takes the remaining length of fabric and flips it around the other shoulder, so that one arm is always covered and the shawl remains stable.

SHE WALKS IN BEAUTY: BRIDAL FOOTWEAR

Did you ever notice how Cinderella's glass shoes were always referred to as "slippers"? Not pumps, mules, or heels, but slippers. The very word implied quiet refinement, a ladylike step, an elegant gait. Perhaps all bridal shoes should be called slippers.

Unless, of course, you're a stiletto, platform, ankle-strap, lace-up boot, or sandal kind of gal. In which case, "slippers" just won't do.

"There is a shoe for every dress," assures Nicole Losurdo, who has served as a shoe expert for hundreds of brides at Kleinfeld. "Bridal shoes have kept up with dress designs and have become much more fashion forward, with embroidery, beading, and even Lucite heels."

Comfort, however, is a major issue. On your wedding day, you'll be dancing, posing for photos, greeting your guests, table hopping, sneaking out back with the bridesmaids . . . in short, being in perpetual motion for eight hours or more. Thus, wedding shoes must be kind as well as beautiful.

"You can spend $29.99 on your shoes," admits Nicole, "but a cheap shoe is a cheap shoe—you'll end up paying in pain." She recommends well-made shoes with kid leather linings and soles, and favors designs by the Grace Collection, Vanessa Noel, Salon Shoes, and Stuart Weitzman. Though they might cost anywhere from $150 to $300, Nicole believes it's money well spent. "They're the best for comfort and stability," she says. "They feel as natural as your own feet."

Kleinfeld bride Agatha Alicandro splurged on her wedding footwear and doesn't regret it. "People thought I was crazy to spend $250 on my shoes," she recalls. "But they were so comfortable, they were worth it."

While you're thinking about shoe styles, think of legwear, too. If you plan to wear stockings or panty hose on your wedding day, then you should steer clear of open toes and avoid sandals that showcase the naked foot. If, on the other hand, you want to display stocking-free feet and ankles, it doesn't mean that you have to forgo supportive underthings: a new generation of "slimwear" can smooth your silhouette while leaving your calves and feet untouched and untethered.

Finally, before shopping for footwear in earnest, think about the types of shoes you're most comfortable in, paying particular attention to heel height. There are very few rigid rules when it comes to adorning the bridal foot. The following are brideworthy shoe styles.

Pump: A pump is a high-heeled shoe of virtually any height that features a closed toe and a closed back. Available in a mind-boggling range of materials and variations, the classic bridal pump—with a heel measuring two inches (or thereabouts)—is appropriate for any sort of wedding. Note: Pumps are preferred by more than 80 percent of Kleinfeld brides.

Open-toed pump: Whether it's a peek-a-boo slit or a full cutaway, toe exposure turns a pump into an open-toed shoe. Though they're perfectly acceptable for most summer weddings, accessories expert Nicole Losurdo thinks they're best worn with slightly more casual bridal wear. "A full-skirted, traditional gown wants closed-toe shoes," she states.

All About Accessories

Slingback: A variation of the pump, slingbacks expose the heel of the foot and are held on by a strap that extends from the body of the shoe. Though they show a bit more skin than the traditional wedding pump, slingbacks are considered to be quite conservative and therefore could be worn for formal or near formal affairs that take place in the warmer months.

Monk: A courtly version of the pump, this closed shoe features a curved heel and a tongue that extends over the arch of the foot, which is often decorated by a bow or other ornament. Highly structured, monks tend to look best with traditional, full-skirted gowns and are particularly suited to fall and winter weddings.

Platform: Platform shoes add height at both the heel and the ball of the foot with the addition of layers of material (cork, wood, and so on). Whether subtle (quarter inch) or daring (an inch or higher), platforms offer an advantage to the active bride: they cushion the foot against the impact of floors, sidewalks, and steps. The trade-off is that platform shoes lack flexibility and can cause a bride's gait to seem clunky. A nontraditional choice, platforms should probably be reserved for select semiformal or informal events, especially since so many of them feature open toes, ankle straps, and other potentially eyebrow-raising details.

Mule: The mule, a backless pump, is a flirtatious shoe that was originally worn by Japanese courtesans and women in

Arab harems. Right up until the mid-1900s, mules were considered to be a kind of lingerie for the feet and were rarely worn outdoors. Today they're everywhere: on the street, in the office, at nightclubs, and, yes, on stylish brides. Classic mules have closed toes, which can make an elegant statement peeking out from under a hem. Be warned, however, that they can be precarious on stairs, on uneven ground, or with certain gowns. "Your foot lifts up in the back," notes Nicole. "If you're wearing a clinging dress, the hem could get caught."

Slipper: Bridal slippers are simple and flat and usually made of luxurious materials like glove-soft leather or satin. They go well with long, voluminous gowns and are often the first choice of brides who are as tall as or taller than their grooms. Like ballet slippers, but with sturdier soles, bridal slippers offer comfort and flexibility and are wonderful to dance in. They tend to lack support and shock absorption, however, and some of the more delicate versions might prove too flimsy for marathon receptions.

Flat: The term *flat* can describe any shoe with a heel that's one inch or less (including the bridal slipper described above). Easy on the feet, bridal flats have become increasingly attractive in recent years thanks to imaginative shoe designers. They're inherently demure and are best matched with full-skirted gowns.

All About Accessories

Sandal: Once considered to be too risqué for brides, elegant sandals—especially high-heeled versions—are now a fashion staple that look wonderful with summery gowns and sophisticated sheaths. Says Kleinfeld's Nicole Losurdo: "If the dress has a naked feel, if it is sexy and slinky, the shoes should be the same." Sandals are rarely worn at ultraformal weddings, and those brides who are planning religious ceremonies should get official approval in advance, since many houses of worship don't welcome brides with exposed skin even on the foot.

Wedding boot: The wedding boot is a high-heeled, ankle-hugging, lace-up boot made of fabric or leather. It tends to be Victorian in spirit—especially when laced with grosgrain ribbon—and can be charming when balanced against a wintry bridal ensemble of any level of formality.

Etc: Nontraditional brides can make up their own rules. In recent years, brides have marched down the aisle in white Doc Martens, decorated sneakers, flat thong sandals (toe rings optional), Roman sandals that lace up the leg, vintage stilettos, high-heeled demiboots, cowboy boots, thigh-high boots, and all sorts of footwear that defies convention or categories.

Shoe Tips

- *The width of a heel has much to do with its comfort factor. Wider heels offer more stability and shock absorption than thin heels.*
- *The most stable high heels feature some sort of "instep strap"—that is, a Mary Jane–like strap that looks decorative while holding your foot securely in place.*
- *If you have sensitive feet, consider buying two pairs of shoes for your wedding: first, a fine, delicate pair to wear during the ceremony, in the receiving line, and for photographs; and second, a sturdier, more comfy pair to take you through hours of carrying on.*
- *Don't take the aisle in a pair of virgin shoes. Before the wedding, wear them around the house or scuff up the soles with some fine sandpaper in order to avoid slipping.*
- *If you're getting married or holding your reception outdoors, you should probably steer clear of shoes made from untreated fabrics, such as brocade. Not only do they absorb moisture, they're also a magnet for grass stains, which can be difficult to remove.*

Shoes to Dye For

An unwritten rule of bridal fashion is that the shoes should always match the gown. The thinking behind the custom is that the preferred wedding shoe not only extends the line of the dress, but is, in fact, an extension of the dress. Though the unconventional bride can certainly choose to ignore this rule, it is true that bright white shoes would stand out in harsh contrast with a cream-colored dress, and ecru shoes would probably look dull or even dingy when paired with a pure white gown.

A number of shoe designers offer brideworthy styles in various shades of white. Though different brands have different color names, Nicole defines the three basic bridal shoe colors as follows:

Stark white: Sometimes called "bright white," this intense, reflective shade tends to have icy blue highlights and is associated with synthetic fabrics.

Diamond white: It might be called "natural white" or "silk white," but it's still a pure white with warm, creamy undertones.

Off-white: This is not just a color, but a category that encompasses the darkest of the whites. Names such as "ivory," "candlelight," "eggshell," "champagne," and others describe off-white shades with subtle tints of gold, blush, buff, beige, and more.

Lots of standard bridal shoe styles are made specifically to be "dyed to match." You can also choose to buy whatever shoes you love and have them custom-dyed. This can be done if 1) the original color is close to your dress color (ivory dye simply won't cover black shoes); 2) the sole of the shoe is light or neutral in color (dark soles can be visually jarring); and 3) the shoe is made of a dyeable material. If you're not sure that your shoes of choice can take a dye, bring them to a reputable shoemaker and find out before you commit.

High-heel Trivia

- In Colonial Massachusetts, a law was passed that forbade women from using high heels—which at the time were imported from Paris—to "seduce or betray" men into acts of matrimony. Any and all "virgins, maidens, or widows" who wore high heels risked being tried and convicted for practicing witchcraft. What's more, any marriage that occurred as a result of high heels would be declared null and void.
- There's a good reason why high heels were, and are, considered sexy: they not only add height, they also raise the buttocks as much as 25 percent and arch the back, pushing the chest forward.
- Catherine de Medici is credited with being the mother of the modern high heel. She modified the "chopine," a kind of platform shoe popular in sixteenth-century Venice, by lowering the ball of the foot and keeping the back of the foot elevated. For hundreds of years thereafter, high heels were associated with privilege and were worn by both men and women of status.

Sneaky Solution

When actress Vivica A. Fox got married in 1998, she opted for a traditional wedding and dressed her six bridesmaids in platinum-toned gowns. But she kept their comfort close to heart. "I didn't want everyone saying, 'Oh, girl, my shoes are so uncomfortable,'" she told People magazine. So she gifted each of her attendants with Reebok sneakers—trimmed in silver to match their dresses—so that after the ceremony they could dance the night away on pain-free feet.

THE CROWNING GLORY: BRIDAL HEADWEAR

A jeweled tiara with a waltz-length veil; a single gardenia tucked into a chignon; a cascade of chiffon topped by a crown of roses: decorative headwear can instantly transform a woman in a white dress into a bride.

Though some mass merchandisers prepackage veils and headpieces with their gowns, most often bridal headwear is sold separately. In the retail world, a bride is free to create her own look by picking and choosing from a delightful assortment of veils, headpieces, hats, and other hair adornments.

According to Christy Kakanakis, Kleinfeld's headpiece manager, a popular bridal adornment right now are hair sticks, which look like highly ornamental chopsticks and are inserted into upswept hairdos. Big, sparkling princess tiaras are in the highest demand," says Christy, "and some brides wear both, so that the tiara sparkles in the front and the hair sticks sparkle at the back."

Celebrities have a profound influence on bridal wear, and right now Christy's department is experiencing Catherine Zeta-Jones mania. As you may recall, the actress was married in a wide, metal-lace tiara that stood almost two inches tall and stretched from ear to ear. "Ever since her wedding to Michael Douglas, people come in and request a Catherine Zeta-Jones headpiece," says Christy.

Today's best-loved headpiece styles include the following:

Tiara: Tiaras started out not as symbols of royalty but as jewelry for the head. "At a gala evening, the invitation would specify that tiaras be worn," explains Christy Kakanakis. "There were all kinds of tiaras—mourning tiaras with black stones, summer tiaras with turquoise and rose quartz, and tiaras that featured a detachable brooch." Today's assortment of bridal tiaras isn't quite as colorful, but is offered in hundreds of styles and sizes. Attached to the head by combs, it might be an exotic crown dripping with gemstones and pearls or a subtle band embellished with crystals and beads.

Starter piece: This updated headpiece is a contemporary variation of the tiara; it measures four to five inches across and is attached (via combs) either at the front of the hairdo or at the top edge of the veil. "Lots of brides want a starter piece that matches the lace on their dresses," says Christy. "We can do that, and we can custom-make pieces designed by the bride."

Headband: This casual headpiece can be as simple as a cloth-covered band that extends from temple to temple, though most modern headbands are jeweled or beaded. Often used to sweep the hair away from the face, headbands are secured by means of short "teeth" rather than combs.

Hair jewelry: Decorative clips that attach to the hair. These can range from tiny, sparkling "picks" to large, elegant barrettes.

Picks and Sticks: Picks are jeweled or ornamental bobby pins. "Sticks" are decorative chopsticks that are inserted in up-'dos.

Wreath: A circular crown of flowers, feathers, leaves, seed pearls, and so on. Crowns can be large enough to encircle the head or small enough to frame a modest bun.

All About Accessories

Juliet cap: A curved, structured cap that hugs the back of the head.

Pillbox: A round, brimless hat worn on the top of the head.

Picture hat: A wide-brimmed hat, often adorned with flowers or other decorations.

Skullcap: An unstructured, brimless cap that closely covers the crown of the head down to the middle of the forehead. Skullcaps are usually made of fabric or lace, though some styles are crocheted.

Profile: A decorative comb enhanced by flowers, netting, or jewels, worn on the side or the back of the head.

Halo: A decorative band that encircles the front of the forehead.

Snood: A woven or net "bag" that captures the hair (which is usually styled in a bun or a chignon) at the nape of the neck.

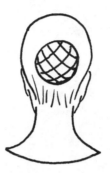

LOVE IN BLOOM

If you are planning on wearing a fresh flower headpiece—or just fresh flowers in your hair—on your wedding day, Kleinfeld headpiece manager Christy Kakanakis has a few words of advice. "Have it designed by a florist," she counsels, "and have two made." Why? Because fresh flowers can—and will—droop and develop brown edges over the course of the day. Her solution? "Keep one refrigerated on site at your reception and make the switch when your original headpiece starts to look tired." Or, as we recommend, use flower buds in your headpiece or your hair, because they last much longer than open blooms.

An alternative to fresh flowers is a silk floral headpiece. At

All About Accessories

Kleinfeld, artisans have matched flower details on dresses and woven them into custom headpieces. But nearly any high-quality silk flowers can, in the hands of professional designers, be fashioned into stunning crowns. If you want fragrance as well as beauty, Christy suggests a mix of fresh and silk. "The greenery can be fresh, and the flowers can be faux," she says, noting that certain kinds of greenery will hold up much longer than fragile blossoms.

HAIRDO'S AND HAIR DON'TS

When it comes to bridal hairstyles, Kleinfeld experts agree on three basic rules:

1. **On your wedding day, you can wear your hair any way you want—as long as it's mostly off your face.**

   Your dress, jewelry, headpiece, and veil are all designed to frame one thing: your face. It is your eyes, your smile, and the blush on your cheeks that will be eagerly watched and endlessly photographed from every angle. So it's folly to obscure any part of your face with curtains of hair. Why do you suppose that most wedding gowns have gorgeous necklines and backlines? They're designed to flatter an exposed neck and an unobstructed face.

   Depending on the length and texture of your hair, you

might want to choose an up-'do, in which the hair is arranged on top of the head in a bun, chignon, modified beehive, or loose pile, with or without decorative hair sticks. If long hair is a signature style you can't live without, try a half-up half-down hairstyle that keeps your hair away from your face but allows it to cascade down your back. Brides with straight, shiny hair might be able to smooth it back and capture it in a simple clip, a sculptural bun, or a collection of jeweled hair clips.

2. **Don't let your hairstyle overwhelm your face.**

Have you ever been to a wedding at which you barely recognized the bride? Sometimes a heavy-handed makeup job is to blame, but more often it's an unnatural hairstyle that makes a bride look like a plastic model of herself. Bundles of cascading curls, a halo of stiff tendrils, extreme hair extensions—these can actually detract from a bride's beauty. If you're tempted to follow a trend or do something dramatic for your wedding day, be absolutely certain that the hairstyle suits your style and doesn't make you look like someone else.

3. **Make sure your hair works with your headpiece, and vice versa.**

There is no tried-and-true formula for matching headpieces with hairstyles, but it is true that certain combinations work better than others. Let your bridal consultant

All About Accessories

lead you in the right direction, and recruit your favorite hairstylist to make your coif harmonize with your headpiece and veil.

THE TALE OF THE VEIL

Historically, the veil's main purpose was to shield the bride's face from the groom, right up until the moment the couple stood on the altar and exchanged vows. "Some orthodox brides still wear what's known as a decté," says Rachel Leah Katz, Kleinfeld's religious bridal consultant. "It's made of the same fabric as the dress, which means that she can't see through it. The mother and the father have to guide her down the aisle. At the end of the ceremony the groom lifts the veil—he's the first to see her."

More often, bridal veils are made of translucent, featherweight fabrics that allow a bride to see where she's going—and glide gracefully down the aisle—and also make it easy for her groom to lift the veil away from her kissable face.

Veils have a certain magic to them. Because their fabric captures light but doesn't block it, they create a visual aura around a bride's face. Longer veils extend that illusion, so that it can seem as if the bride has her own personal aurora borealis trailing behind her. What's good for the ceremony isn't necessarily right for the reception, however. And so we have detachable veils. These are easily removed from headpieces so that the bride may enjoy her party without fear of having her veil stepped on or otherwise damaged.

According to Mary Meitanis, another good reason to opt for a detachable veil has to do with photo opportunities. "If you're wearing a veil during profile shots—cutting your cake, or kissing your husband—all you see is a veil and a nose," she points out. "The night only lasts eight hours, but your photos are forever."

The majority of contemporary veils are made of tulle or organza. Some have rolled edges (the edges of the fabric are literally hand-rolled), while others are "machine edged" (the veil is hemmed with tiny stitches). But most veils aren't edged at all. Why? Because the airy, diaphanous look of a veil is lost when it's framed by a hem or piping. Anyway, says Christy, the finished edges don't photograph well. "They appear as prominent lines," she notes.

That doesn't mean veils have to be plain. Use your imagination. Veils are lovely when enhanced with embroidery or appliqués; decorated with bugle beads, crystals, or sequins; or dotted with sparkling rhinestones.

Popular veil styles include the following:

Cathedral: The longest of the traditional veils, these usually accompany a cathedral-length train and fall about 3½ yards from the headpiece.

Chapel: This somewhat shorter veil is often paired with a chapel-length train and measures about 2½ yards from the headpiece.

Ballet or waltz: A veil that falls to the ankles.

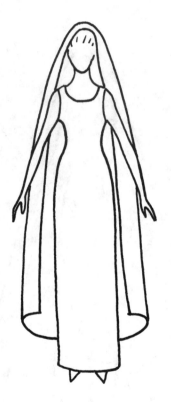

Fingertip: As the name suggests, this veil's hem grazes the fingertips when the arms are held straight at the sides.

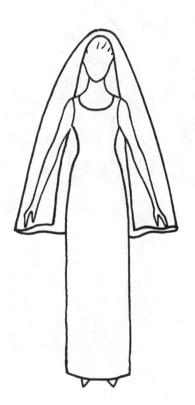

Waterfall: A multilayered veil that brushes the shoulders.

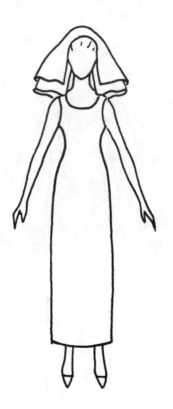

Blusher: A short, single-layer veil that is worn forward over the bride's face before the ceremony and is then pushed backward after the ceremony. Often it is layered over a second, longer veil that remains fixed at the back.

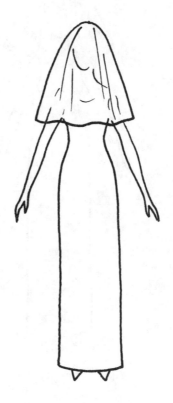

Pouf: A short, decorative gathering of veiling, usually attached to a headpiece.

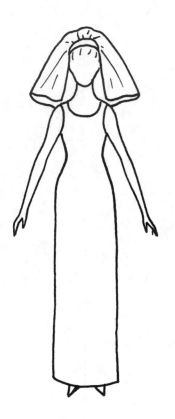

Angel: A flat, square-cut, ungathered veil that's most often worn with contemporary, minimalist-style gowns and simple headpieces.

Bird cage: A stiff, shoulder-length veil whose edges are tacked to a comb or hat to create a birdcage-like shape. The bird cage veil is most often attached to a small hat such as a pillbox.

Mantilla: Virtually the only veil designed to be worn without a headpiece in modern times, the mantilla is a simple drape of lace. "Although they're a Spanish tradition, mantillas are extremely popular," reports Mary Moitanis, custom headpiece artisan. "They are placed on a bride's head, draped over a high, elaborate comb. They're often family heirlooms, passed down through generations. One might be made from the skirt of a bride's mother's wedding gown, which in turn can become part of a christening outfit, and so on."

Circular veil: A very modern veil, the circular veil has no gathering and attaches to the head with a flat comb. It can be any length, but when worn long it looks like your body is swathed in tulle. This style looks great with a simple sheath.

THAT CERTAIN SPARKLE: THE BRIDE AND HER JEWELRY

Like most grown women, you are probably an expert when it comes to accessorizing with jewelry. You know about balancing earrings with hairstyles; enhancing necklines with chokers, strands, chains, or pendants; creating interest with bracelets and rings; and personalizing outfits with clips and brooches.

Successful bridal accessorizing requires similar skills, but with a new set of challenges. In most cases, the bride's task is to find jewelry that harmonizes with the decorative details on her headpiece, veil, bodice, sleeves, gloves, train, and skirt. Keep in mind that white gowns are usually matched with pure white and silver-toned pieces; off-white and ivory gowns are paired with creamy white and gold-toned accessories. (Luckily, every shade of gown goes with "clear"—the color of diamonds.)

Given these narrow options, it makes sense that bridal jewelry collections are dominated by sweet, discreet pieces made with pearls, diamonds (real or synthetic), pavé, crystals, and/or tiny, iridescent beads.

Is there room in this jewelry box for personal expression? Of course. You're free to jazz up your look with unexpected pieces or go completely without jewels. Of course, tradition and sentiment always prevail.

Here at Kleinfeld, we have a mantra: "Nothing on the neck!"

All About Accessories

It's not that we're anti-jewelry. It's just that we consider certain territory to be sacred. Stand back and take a look: The bride's body is swathed in white silk, while the top of her head is adorned with jewels and yards of tulle. In between is her face, her neck, and her upper chest—all natural, all naked, all beautiful. Sculptors of olden days focused on this area and carved what we now call classical busts. They thought of the chest, neck, and head as a single unit that comprised the most precious and expressive part of a person. And so do we.

We don't want anything to interrupt that graceful symmetry, that poetic geometry, and so we advise most brides to avoid necklaces and wear the tiniest of earrings. When there's too much to look at, you can't see the bride, right? But it is the exception that makes the rule. And when it comes to the betrothed and her jewelry, there are plenty of exceptions. Consider the following options:

Earrings. Earring choices are dictated by three major factors. First: your hairstyle. Short cuts, tall updos, or any style that exposes the ear and the neck practically begs for earrings. Second: your headwear. Generally speaking, simple headpieces call for simple earrings, while large or elaborate headpieces are well balanced by substantial earrings that continue the theme of the headpiece. The relationship between veils and earrings is a bit more complicated, because veils come in so many styles and lengths. The goal is to balance the visual weight of your headpiece and hairdo without detracting from the sweep of the veil.

Third: the neckline of your gown. Low-cut, sleeveless, and halter-top gowns look wonderful with drop earrings, while gowns with high necks, collars, or design details around the shoulders and throat are usually better with short earrings that don't interrupt the line of the shoulder.

Necklaces. Kleinfeld experts generally advise against them, but necklaces have held an important part in bridal attire for years. Whether it's a short strand of Grandma's Mikimoto pearls or an exotic splash of sparkling gems, necklaces can be counted on to draw attention to the bride's face and upper body. They work best against bare skin and can add polish to square, scoop, sweetheart, Sabrina, and portrait necklines. Necklaces should be chosen with great care, however, because many of today's gowns have sculpted bodices that are de-signed to elongate the neck and flatter the bust—an effect that can be erased by an imposing or poorly positioned necklace. But embellishments are up to you—chosen with intelligence, of course.

Chokers. True chokers encircle the neck and shouldn't be confused with short necklaces that rest at the base of the throat. The choker can be as demure as a simple ribbon dan-gling a small pendant or as dramatic as a wide, diamond-studded collar. In any case, chokers tend to flatter tall women with long necks and are most successful when paired with low-cut dresses.

All About Accessories

Bracelets. Though they are not traditional bridal accessories, certain sleeveless and strapless gowns can be greatly enhanced by bracelets worn on one or both wrists. Avoid bangle bracelets, loose-fitting bracelets, or any bracelet with pendants or charms. Why? They're noisy. Clattering metal is probably not what you want to hear as your beloved nervously slips a ring on your finger.

Rings. On your wedding day, your engagement ring and your wedding band should shine like stars, without competition from other rings on either hand. You're allowed to break this rule only if the interloping ring has a deeply sentimental or symbolic meaning. Note: You might consider having your engagement ring cleaned before the wedding.

Watches: Never wear one on your wedding day. A bride shouldn't be aware of the minutes or the hours—after all, it's a timeless day.

ALL YOU NEED IS GLOVES

There was a time when a true lady wouldn't dream of leaving her house without gloves, no matter what the season. Gloves came in specific sizes and styles: there were wrist-length gloves to wear to church and luncheons, evening-length gloves for cocktail parties, and opera-length gloves for formal affairs.

Slowly, over the last four decades or so, dress gloves faded away and nearly became extinct. Toward the end of the last century, it seemed that only First Ladies at inaugural balls and singers on cruise ships wore long gloves with their evening gowns.

Happily, forward-thinking brides of this shiny new millennium are reviving the tradition of the dress glove. There are a number of good reasons for loving gloves right now, and most of them have to do with the fact that there's a new breed of gloves made (at least partially) from stretchy synthetics. This means that even extralong gloves fit beautifully and remain smoothly in place for hours and hours.

Whatever shape your arms are in, gloves lend an air of for-

Gloves vs. Rings

If you plan to wear long gloves for your ceremony, you're faced with a quandary: How do you exchange rings? Though you may encounter advice about making a slit in your glove's ring finger or slipping your hand out of the buttoned wrist of your glove, these options are neither practical nor attractive. The best solution is the simplest: remove your gloves at the altar and hand them to your maid of honor, an attendant, or your mother.

After you've said, "I do," you can don your gloves as needed—for formal photographs, the first dance, the cake cutting—or you can ignore them altogether and show off your wedding band instead.

---

mality. A ballerina-style dress becomes a ball gown; a cocktail dress becomes formal wear; and a backless, strapless sheath might look respectable enough for a church wedding.

Your glove glossary:

Opera: The longest, most formal glove; extends to the upper arm. Tina Gatto, Kleinfeld's assistant bridal manager, likes them with strapless gowns, but even with sleeveless styles, they're very Jackie O.

Short: Gloves that end at the wrist or just above the wrist. Short gloves are suitable for less formal affairs and tend to have a springtime look.

Evening: Also called "midlength," these gloves rise just above the elbow.

Gauntlet: A long, fingerless glove that ends in a V shape at the hand, where it attaches by a loop to a single finger.

TO HAVE AND TO HOLD: WEDDING PURSES

We're living in the era of the evening purse. Have they ever been more stunning, whimsical, or collectible than they are right now? There is a rich and delicious assortment of small, sparkling bags that would no doubt be a fabulous addition to your bridal ensemble. Unfortunately, you, as a bride, are not permitted to carry one. That is the job of your maid of honor or perhaps your mother.

Generally, bridal purses fall into two categories: the personal clutch or evening bag, in which the bride stashes her lipstick, emergency repair kit, tissues, and so on. Again, this bag is usually toted around by a designated purse carrier, except when the bride visits the ladies' room. Though the purse might not get much attention, every bride needs one that looks great with her ensemble and can easily hold her essentials.

The second type of bag is known as a "money bag" and is designed to hold envelopes full of cash and checks bestowed by generous friends and loved ones. The money bag ritual, in which the bride and groom go from table to table to greet their guests and discreetly collect their loot, is something of an old world custom. Whether you cherish the tradition or not, you should know that a money purse is a soft-sided bag with a drawstring handle that the bride wears around her wrist. It's usually made of some luxurious fabric that matches—or at least complements—the wedding gown and is large enough to accommodate wedding card–size envelopes. In some families it's customary for the bride's purse to be handmade by one of her relatives. However, attractive models are also available in the retail market.

UNDERNEATH IT ALL: UNDERGARMENTS

In the strange and curious land of bridal wear, underthings are not mere bras, panties, slips, or teddies: they are foundation garments. Beyond making your body look toned, smooth, and supported, their task is to provide a kind of exoskeleton upon which a weighty, ornate dress can be hung. Upscale bridal salons—like Kleinfeld—usually offer an assortment of specialty undergarments that you can try before you buy. However, if you have your undergarments made professionally by a corsetier, then have her prepare a proper bra for the exact style of your wedding dress. It pays to be an informed consumer, especially at this time in your life.

Here's what you need to know:

Bras. No matter what style of gown you choose, your wedding day bust must be well defined and well supported. Unless you have gravity-proof breasts and/or implants, you'll need a smooth, structured bra that is undetectable under your dress. Strapless gowns call for strapless bras; backless gowns require bras that hook at the back of the waist; and low-cut necklines, designed to frame womanly charms, will probably look best with padded bras. Be warned, however, that some bras can cut into the torso and create an unsightly crease under the bust or across the back. If this is the case, it's time to move on to bustiers.

Bustiers. The bustier is more or less a long-line bra that supports your bosom while tightening your upper torso. The bustier's main advantage is that it creates a clean, crease-free line between the bust and the waist. Many strapless and/or backless gowns look most attractive with a bustier underneath.

Sew-Ins. Some brides might benefit from padded cups sewn directly into the lining of the dress. Sew-ins work best with structured bodices, but you should ask your consultant or fitter for guidance.

Half Bra. A backless bra that clings to the front of the torso and stays up by virtue of adhesive applied to the sides of the rib cage.

Unbras. What if you're wearing a halter dress or other clingy, skin-baring gown? The "unbra" (sold under various brand names) consists of a pair of flesh-colored foam cups that adhere directly to your skin. They're designed to promote a shapely, symmetrical silhouette and obscure prominent nipples. Not everybody is a fan of the unbra, however. Nitsa Glezelis, director of alterations, says, "These things don't really stay on and don't give much support." Her advice: "If you're small, and you need to disguise your nipples, just use little round Band-Aids."

Slimmers. Old-fashioned girdles were horribly heavy, cumbersome, and restraining. Luckily we have newfangled slimmers that are lightweight, flexible, and available in a whole range of flaw-correcting styles. Heavy thighs? Try a slimmer that extends from the waist to the knees. Saggy behind? Buy a slimmer designed to reshape and uplift your posterior.

Whatever your problem area, it's likely you can find a slimmer that works for you.

Slips. Some gowns—and some bodies—don't require corrective undergarments. However, many dresses look and feel better when they're draped over a silky slip that extends from the shoulders or the bust all the way down to the ankles. Because slips are inherently comfortable, they may be the right choice for brides who want complete freedom of movement but need to smooth over blips and bulges here and there. In any case, they're essential for gowns that aren't 100 percent opaque.

Panties. Nothing can ruin the look of a wedding gown faster than visible panty lines—except, maybe, a bride who is constantly tugging at her creeping underwear. If you're going to be encased in layers of slips, slimming garments, panty hose, and the like, you might consider abandoning panties altogether. If you really need them, shop for flesh-colored panties that hug the body but don't crawl or make cuts in the waist or legs.

Hosiery. Control-top panty hose might not be your favorite type of undergarment. Yet control-tops can be a godsend, because they offer leg coverage and hip and stomach improvement in one handy package. If you opt instead to wear a garter belt and thigh-high stockings, make sure the belt fits snugly around your waist and is secured at the back with hooks, so that it doesn't slip down during the course of the evening. Whatever your choice, be sure to have spare hosiery on hand. Even ultracivilized brides have been known to sprout holes and runs when they least expect them. One final note: Bridal hosiery, like bridal jewelry, comes in only a few colors: white, off-white, and clear.

Nothing. Of all the new trends that have recently emerged in the bridal undergarment industry, perhaps the most shocking is nothing. It's true: many hard-bodied brides are choosing to walk down the aisle in gowns so figure clinging that the only foundation garment they could possibly wear is skin. If it looks good and feels good, go for it. But first heed the advice of bridal experts: Get a thorough, professional wax job.

All About Accessories

Chapter Six

Your Fitting

A fitting is a specialized process that takes place whenever an article of clothing is special-ordered. Remember, even though your dress is specially ordered from the designer, it is still a stock size and will require a couple of fittings. In bridal salon vernacular, the fitter (usually a seamstress, dressmaker, or tailor) is a highly skilled artisan who, over the course of many hours or several months, transforms a dress not only into a custom-made garment but *your* wedding gown.

Brides who buy their gowns at full-service salons almost always have their fittings done in-house. Smaller salons may have fitters who service customers on a freelance basis, perhaps at a separate location.

The bride who buys off the rack or isn't working directly with a salon may have to find her own source for fittings and alterations. If this describes your situation, be sure to choose a seamstress or tailor who specializes in bridal wear. This is important because 1) wedding gowns are more complex than the average garment; 2) they're made of extraordinarily fine, delicate, and/or fragile fabrics; and 3) they must be fully taken apart in order to make adjustments, then put back together—beading, edging, lace, ruffles, embroidery, gathered skirts, and all.

Basic bridal gown fitting procedures include adjusting the hem of the skirt and fine-tuning the fit of the sleeves, neckline, and bodice. Most gowns can be adjusted to perfection within three fittings. Beyond basic fittings are alterations that customize your dress. Do you want to have a long-sleeved dress made into a short-sleeved dress? Do you want to get rid of those spaghetti straps and replace them with something at least as wide as fettuccine? Do you want to soften a scooped back with a panel of illusion lace? Various additions and subtractions are possible, depending on the dress, but it is your fitter who will determine which procedures can be done successfully and which can't.

THE BASIC FITTINGS SCHEDULE

First Fitting

This is the day you've been waiting for. Your one true gown has been delivered to the salon. The pictures in your head are about to become real, and you are about to try on a dress that's been created just for you and has never been tried on before. Your first fitting can be a celebration, if you so choose;

many brides invite close friends and family to this happy event. But be advised that fittings are also serious business. To make the most of this and subsequent appointments, bring along your wedding shoes, bridal undergarments (the bra is especially important), headpiece and veil, and a camera or a videocamera to capture the moment.

Ann Nicosia, director of operations and customer service, loves the excitement that builds up when a bride is about to see her wedding gown for the first time. "Some of the brides don't quite remember what the dress looks like, because it's been months since they ordered it," says Darlyn. "Then the fitter carries it down the hall, turns the corner, and the bride says, "Oh, my God! That's my dress! That's my dress!' "

"Some brides don't recognize their gowns at first," says Nitsa Glezelis, director of alterations at Kleinfeld. "They see it on the hanger and they're sure it's not theirs," she says. "It looks different because of what's been built up in their minds. But they they try it on, and by the end of the session they're convinced it's their gown."

The first fitting is not only your introduction to your wedding gown; it's also your introduction to your fitter and the beginning of a special bond. In fact, many brides invite their fitters to their weddings. In most top salons, the same fitter will work with a bride from the first fitting to the last, so it is important that you feel comfortable with the artisan assigned to you.

Your first fitting is also the time for a little dress aerobics. Lean

A Case of Colorful Amnesia

"I had gotten engaged in July 2000, and wanted to get married in the spring," says Lauren Silverman. "Then I decided a long engagement would drive me crazy, and we moved the date to January." When the impatient bride and her mother made an appointment to visit Kleinfeld, Lauren hadn't the slightest idea of what style wedding gown she wanted. "My mom made me look through magazines," she says. "I found an ad I liked, and brought it with me. It turns out Kleinfeld carried the exact same dress. I ended up buying it."

The gown was unusual in that it was detailed with colored beads. "Color had just been introduced to bridal dresses," says Lauren. "This one was a peachy ivory tone, strapless, with a thin satin bow around the waist, and it had pale lilac, pink, and yellow beading worked into a discreet flower motif. I loved it."

A rush order was put on the dress, and it was delivered to Kleinfeld in December. The bride-to-be invited her parents to the first fitting; they arrived in high spirits and with a video camera. "My mom gave me a warning," Lauren remembers. "She said, 'Don't be upset if the gown doesn't look exactly the same as you remember.'" Mrs. Silverman's maternal intuition, as it turns out, was directly on target. "I tried it on, and I hated it," says Lauren of her chosen gown. "It just didn't look the same to me. I actually said, 'I'm not taking this dress.'"

In a state of panic, Lauren started rifling through sample dresses, which were her only option if she wanted to be married in January. "I called my fiancé in tears and told him we were going to have to postpone the wedding," she says. His response was at once loving and astute: "He told me I'd look beautiful even if I wore a potato sack."

Lauren's mother, with a heroic assist from Mara, managed to gently turn the crisis around. "First, my mother tried on the dress, and I got a good look at it," says Lauren. "Then Mara took me upstairs and put me in a deluxe dressing room. The lighting was better. I changed my hair, and they put a matching veil on my head and shoes on my feet." Lauren started to cheer up. When the fitter arrived and pinned the dress to her exact shape, her spirits soared. "I felt magical at that moment," she recalls. "I felt for the first time that I was getting married. Plus, my mom started to cry. That's how I knew it was the right dress."

Five hours later, the gown was Lauren's own. "Kleinfeld made a circular veil for me that was full in the front and the back, and went all the way down to the floor," she says. "When I walked down the aisle, my dress sparkled; it was different and beautiful, and you couldn't tell until you were up close that it had colored beading." On January 27, 2001, Lauren Silverman became Lauren Kolker, but as far as her wedding gown is concerned, time has stood still: "To this day I get compliments on it," she says.

forward (does anything fall out or look a bit too racy?). Sit down (can you still breathe? is there any unsightly or uncomfortable bunching?). Raise your arms over your head (don't forget, you'll be throwing a bouquet). Slow dance with your shopping companion (can you move easily? are you tripping on the skirt?). Stick your stomach out (do you still look like the belle of the ball?). Walk down an imaginary aisle (does the dress move with you and hang well?). Voice any and all concerns to your fitter immediately. Communication is essential. Nitsa Glezelis remembers one bride who came back, again and again to have her gown adjusted. It wasn't until her fifth visit that she admitted to her fitter that, though she loved the way her gown looked on her, it was so tight she couldn't breathe.

As you're leaving your first fitting, make an appointment for your second, which should take place about a month before your wedding date (unless you're having extensive alterations, in which case ask your seamstress and/or bridal consultant about timing).

Second Fitting

Now that basic alterations have been made during the first fitting, it's time to fine-tune the fit during the second fitting. Adjustments may or may not be minor, but the second fitting presents a great opportunity for you to make major decisions on the details of your bridal ensemble. In addition to your

The Incredible Growing Bride vs. the Incredible Shrinking Bride

Professional fitters are experts at making a gown fit your body. But what if, between your first fitting and the day of your wedding, your body changes radically?

It's all part of the adventure, says Nitsa Glezelis, Kleinfeld's director of alterations. She encounters many brides who insist that they're going to lose weight before their weddings. "We'll order a size sixteen dress for a size twenty bride, but she has to take responsibility for it," says Nitsa. "She has to sign a piece of paper that says she'll pay for the smaller dress, whether she actually loses the weight or not."

Sometimes weight loss comes as a surprise. Nitsa tells the story of one plus-size bride who ordered an oversized dress. "The pattern had to be made especially for her, and it cost an additional $700," says Nitsa. Between the time that the dress was ordered, designed, and delivered to Kleinfeld, the bride lost nearly fifty pounds. "She wanted to cancel production, but it was too late," Nitsa says. "So my department had to reconstruct the dress to fit her new shape." Because the change was so drastic, the dress had to be totally taken apart and virtually remade, piece by piece, bead by bead, crystal by crystal.

Pregnancy is also a size issue that Kleinfeld's fitters have had plenty of experience with over the years. "Sometimes a girl doesn't know she's pregnant when she orders her dress," says Nitsa. "so we have to work with the dress she's got. We'll order more fabric from the designer, open *it up, add panels—whatever it takes." Nitsa says an even greater chal-lenge is when a bride comes in a few months pregnant and wants to get married shortly after she has her child. "We have to do the math," says Nitsa with a good-natured smile.*

Obviously. it's much easier for any fittings department to create a good fit on a stable-sized body. If you're pregnant, or think you might be, let your fitter know, so that specialized alterations can be arranged in ad-vance.

headpiece, veil, and shoes, bring along your jewelry, gloves, shawls, bag, and other accessories. Some brides like to do "hair trials" at this time and might have their hair styled for this occasion or simply pack various hair clips in order to ap-proximate hairstyles. In any case, it's smart to bring along a camera so you can contemplate your options later. (Note: All salons allow cameras to be used during the fitting process.)

Before you schedule your next fitting, consult with your seam-stress to see how many more appointments will be required. Schedule as many as you need. The additional time spent with your fitter will be well rewarded on your wedding day.

Final Fitting

Don't attend your final fitting alone: your maid of honor or mother should come along in order to learn the special re-

The Bride Wore Ivory

Jennifer Parris wasn't your average Kleinfeld bride. "My son was two months old when I started looking for my wedding dress," she explains. "It was July 2000, and I was getting married in September. Buying a dress was just something I had to get done."

Jennifer was actually on her second round of wedding gown shopping. She was originally to be married on June 17, 2000, to the man she'd been with for thirteen years. At that time, she was disappointed by the various salons she visited. "The people were really pushy, they all had the attitude of sell, sell sell," she recalls. "One of them offered me a dress for $2,000, which was $500 off the ticket price. I said, 'I need to go outside and think about it first.' The salesperson said, 'If you leave the store now, even for a minute, I'm going to charge you full price.' It wasn't the way I wanted to buy my wedding dress."

Her shopping stopped abruptly when Jennifer got an even more urgent deadline: she became pregnant and learned that her due date was June 7, ten days before her wedding date. She did the sensible thing and postponed her wedding.

Fast forward to July 2000. With an infant at home and just two months to replan her special day, the very tired Jennifer went to Kleinfeld. "I expected the same treatment at Kleinfeld that I'd gotten at other salons, but instead my experience there was just amazing. My consultant was young and looked like Courteney Cox; and Kleinfeld had a makeup artist and hairstylist there, who did my hair and makeup really fast, free of charge.

"I told my consultant that I was looking for something to hide the fact that I just had a baby. She brought me three dresses, and the first one was really the right one. The others were more expensive, but she told me the first one looked best on me, and it made me trust her more.

As it turned out, the dress that Jennifer loved was designed by Christos—who was making a rare personal appearance at Kleinfeld for his trunk show. "Christos dressed and bustled me and worked with me in front of the mirror. When he placed the veil on my head, it was a magical moment."

The Kleinfeld staff encouraged Christos to make a Herculean effort to have Jennifer's dress created and delivered on time. "Since I ordered my dress so close to my wedding date," she says, "it was set to arrive about five days before my wedding, and it did. I had to have a one-day fitting, but I was never worried because Kleinfeld kept in touch every step of the way."

The dress was ivory toned, with spaghetti straps and beading. "There was one thing I swore I'd never have on my dress—a bow," says Jennifer. "I wanted to look like a bride, not like a meringue. But my consultant talked me into it. She said, 'Everyone's going to be looking at you from the back; it will look too plain.' So I ended up with a big, beaded bow, and now I like it.

"The dress is what really got me excited about the wedding," she continues. "At home I kept peeking at it. All the beads were glistening, it was beautiful. My fiancé kept trying to sneak a look. I wouldn't let him see it."

At the wedding, Jennifer walked down the aisle with her baby boy, who was dressed in a tiny tuxedo. Later, while dancing for the first time with her new husband, she looked up and there was Ronnie, smiling in the doorway. "I started crying," recalls Jennifer. The ever-helpful Ronnie bustled her dress for her, then danced with the bride.

Your Fitting

United They Stand

Among the ranks of the hundred-plus detail divas at Kleinfeld are three who inspect the dresses that come in and the dresses that go out.

One is receiving manager Amelia Allen. Her full-time job is to receive and inspect every shipment that arrives at the store, including gowns, veils, shoes, fabric, beads, undergarments and more. Amelia is well trained for the job—she served as a supplies specialist for the U.S. Army for ten years before signing on with Kleinfeld. "I return merchandise to vendors that is not up to the Kleinfeld quality standards."

Next in line is Darlyn Rios, assistant manager of alterations. "I inspect all newly arrived dresses for flaws or damage and make sure that the measurements are correct," she says. Darlyn has diverted her share of potential disasters, but one in particular stands out. "A wedding dress was delivered with a satin bodice," she recalls. "Silk organza was requested on the order form, so we were able to return the gown and have it fixed before the bride had any idea of the manufacturer's error. She ended up being the happiest bride I'd ever seen."

Once a wedding gown has been fitted, altered, adjusted, and pressed it's subject to the scrutiny of the formidable Bessie Andreakos. She is Kleinfeld's quality control manager, and it is she who inspects every dress before it leaves with a bride. "I check everything, inside and out," says Bessie. "I make sure it's clean and that the seams are perfect. I check every thread, every bead, every button, loop, hook, all the details on veils, gowns, trains, and crinolines. My daughter, Julie, got married this year

> and she looked gorgeous. I inspected her dress the same way I inspect all the dresses at Kleinfeld."
>
> Not all brides are fortunate enough to have Amelia, Darlyn, and Bessie on their side. But we hope that your chosen bridal salon will enforce standards of quality with the same passion as these dedicated women.

quirements of your dress. Straps, buttons, bustles, hooks . . . all of these will need to be commandeered on the day of your wedding.

PICKUP DAY

There are two schools of thought regarding gown pickup. Some brides choose to pick up their gown as close to the wedding date as possible, so that it can remain in the hands of professionals—and away from possible disasters—until it's ready to be worn. There's wisdom in this method, because disasters can and do happen. Dogs, cats, kids, birds, hamsters—none of them are friends to your dress. We know of one bride whose very young brother added his own "decorations" to his sister's gown with a permanent marker the day before the wedding. Another Kleinfeld bride hung her dress at home under an air-conditioning unit that leaked all night. After eight hours the dress was saturated and badly stained. In both cases we removed the stains perfectly.

Your Fitting

Customizing Your Wedding Gown

In addition to fittings and alterations, why not make your special gown even more special with a personal touch or two? Kleinfeld artisans have customized many a dress over the years, ranging from colorful accents— a gown lined entirely in red fabric—to private messages—the words "I love you" embroidered in blue silk on a crinoline. Let your imagination be your guide.

Some ideas:

- Have your own initials and those of your husband's, or your family crest, embroidered into the lining of your dress.
- Carry a handkerchief embroidered with a special message or symbol.
- Have a pocket sewn into the inside hem of your skirt to hold a small sentimental object, such as a talisman, a rosary, a photograph, or a letter from your loved one.
- Personalize the trim on your gown. Caroline Kennedy had shamrocks sewn on her dress's bodice, skirt, and lining in order to pay homage to her family's heritage.
- Honor your ethnic roots with decorative touches that echo homeland traditions.

Some suggestions:

cowry shells (Africa)

feathers (Armenia)

a tiny silver horseshoe, traditionally sewn into the hem of the gown (England)

a silk shawl (Finland)

> *a painted fan (France)*
>
> *gold and silver vines, intertwined (Greece)*
>
> *evergreen branches (Holland)*
>
> *flower petals (India)*
>
> *ribbons (Italy)*
>
> *angels (Java)*
>
> *ducks or geese (Korea)*
>
> *a crown (Norway)*
>
> *doves (Philippines)*
>
> *mother-of-pearl (Samoa)*
>
> *a tartan sash (Scotland)*
>
> *thirteen coins (Spain)*
>
> *myrtle (Latvia and Wales)*

Fearless brides can opt to pick up their gowns two weeks before the event or even sooner. This way they can try on the gown in the salon one last time to make sure it's perfect and can make last-minute adjustments for prewedding weight gain or loss. For these brides, just having the gown in their possession gives them peace of mind.

What if, in spite of your best efforts, your gown becomes creased or wrinkled right before the wedding? Bessie Andreakos, Kleinfeld's quality control manager, offers a remedy: Blow-dry the dress with a hand-held dryer from the inside on a low setting.

Your Fitting

Something Old, Something New, Something Borrowed, Something Blue . . .

" . . . and a silver sixpence in your shoe." This rhyme started in Victorian England and has been a treasured ritual of American and European brides ever since.

- Something old . . . traditionally represents a bride's link with her family, such as her grandmother's locket, her mother's pearls, an heirloom diamond fashioned into a pendant, and so on. Meaningful mementos don't have to be worn, however: some brides may choose to tuck something old into the bridal bouquet, like a vintage handkerchief embroidered by a relative.
- Something new . . . marks the beginning of married bliss, the start of a new life. This one's easy; chances are you'll be wearing all sorts of new items.
- Something borrowed . . . represents the relationship between a bride and her friends or sisters. Custom dictates that the borrowed item be lent by a happily married friend or sibling, then returned after the ceremony. Purses, jewelry, and accessories are often favorite items to borrow.
- Something blue . . . is a symbol of the bride's fidelity that dates back to biblical times, when a bride wore a blue ribbon in her hair to show that she'd always be true. Today, blue garters abound, but there are perhaps more interesting options. Blue flowers in the bouquet, blue lining in the skirt or bodice of the gown, or blue buckles or ornaments on the bridal shoes are all possibilities.

• *Silver sixpence in your shoe . . . is meant to bring wealth, happiness, and joy to the bride and her groom. Today, brides carry on this tradition by placing a penny in the toe of each shoe: one minted in the year of her birth, the other minted in the year of her groom's birth.*

Your Fitting

Kelly's Shining Moment

"I like the whole idea of preserving a wedding gown," says Kelly Gaffey, who became Kelly Skolnick in August 2001. "I want my gown to be as beautiful as the day I wore it, and I would want my daughter to feel the same way I felt on that day—like a princess."

Kelly, who designs handbags for Steve Madden and other impressive houses of style, started her gown search by visiting a Manhattan salon and becoming infatuated with a medieval-type gown that had long, poet-style sleeves. "My mom said I looked as though I were wearing pajamas," recalls Kelly. "She's from Brooklyn and was really pushing Kleinfeld. I went to appease her."

Once inside Kleinfeld's doors, Kelly was enchanted. "My consultant was wonderful," she says. "I had photos with me from magazines, and she brought me one of the exact dresses I'd cut out." The gown was strapless, tight in the bodice and hips, and fishtailed out below the knees. "It was the very first dress I put on, and my mom said, 'That's it.' Suddenly there was a whirlwind of people congratulating me. My mom had made a decision. She had run to the counter and put a down payment on it."

It was all too quick for Kelly, who was dazed and confused. "I started to cry on the way home," she says. "I felt that I'd made the worst mistake of my life." She wrote a letter to Kleinfeld and had them cancel the order. "They were great about it," says Kelly. She made an appointment to go back three weeks later and try on different dresses.

You can guess what happened next: Kelly fell in love with the very gown she'd rejected from her first visit.

"My consultant came to every fitting," Kelly recalls. "She doesn't work on Saturdays, and all my fittings were on Saturdays. She came specially by bus. At my last fitting, she bought me earrings to go with my gown. My mother and I started crying. I actually invited her to my wedding."

On the day that Kelly walked down the aisle in her full ensemble—gown, jeweled choker, veil, headpiece, and earrings—the impact was palpable. "My husband loved it," she says. "My dad cried. It was the reaction you always dream of, like you read about in books."

Your Fitting

Chapter Seven

A Wedding Gown Is Forever

Your dress has taken you through a profound day. A day that, in the timeline of your life, marks the moment when you joined with another to become a couple, a family, a dynasty.

So what will you pass down to future generations? Good genes, certainly. Your wedding rings, most likely. And the fabulous gown that helped make you a memorable bride.

Photographs are a precious record. But if you truly want to preserve the moment and the memory, you must preserve the dress. It's a priceless work of art, is it not? In order to keep it as beautiful as it was on your special day, it needs special care. And that means hiring a wedding gown preservationist. This skilled professional will protect your dress with a series of "archival" treatments, then package it in such a way that it's immune to the ravages of light, dust, body oils, and time.

PRESERVATION 101

The preservation process begins with a gentle dry cleaning, and in fact some dry cleaners offer gown preservation services. Don't just pick a name out of the Yellow Pages, however, and don't blindly hire the lowest bidder. Gown preservation is a specialized procedure that can—and should—cost hundreds of dollars and be executed with the utmost care.

The best preservationists will:

- Clean the gown and veil—without using bleach or other harsh cleaning agents—and free them of acids, alkalis, and sugars, thus creating a neutral (pH7) balance in the fibers.
- Layer the garments, inside and out, with acid-free tissue paper.
- Fold the garments into an archival storage box that's lined with specially treated muslin, which acts as a mothproofer and moisture stabilizer. True archival boxes are acid-, alkali-, and lignin-free and do not have a viewing window.
- Include a pair of conservator gloves to be worn by you when you want to open the box and view your gown.
- Offer a written warranty.

A Wedding Gown Is Forever

DOING YOUR PART

Wedding gown preservation starts almost immediately after the reception. In fact, it should start the minute you peel off, climb out of, or otherwise remove the dress from your body, at which point you're advised to follow these steps:

Hang It Up. Your wedding gown will ultimately be boxed for storage. When you first take it off, however, it should be hung on a padded hanger to be aired out. Keep it out of the closet, away from other garments, and don't cover it in plastic—this will trap vapors and moisture. If the skirt of the gown is exceptionally heavy, drape it on a second hanger and elevate it, in order to prevent the shoulders of the gown from stretching or sagging. Keep your veil on a separate hanger away from the dress, because its delicate fabric can easily snag on beads and sequins.

Get Thee to a Preservationist. You should put your gown into the hands of professionals as soon as possible—such as the day after the ceremony. Time is of the essence, because many stains aren't visible right away. Champagne, for instance, dries clear but later oxidizes and becomes a brown spot, while skin oils and perspiration can settle into a fabric and cause permanent damage. If you're flying away on your honeymoon, arrange for your maid of honor or other responsible person to deliver your gown to the preservationist.

Drive Safely. When ferrying your dress to and from your hotel, home, or preservationist, wrap it in a clean, undyed cotton or muslin sheet and lay it flat. Again, keep it separate from your veil and other accessories.

Store It Right. Your preserved gown needs to be kept in a cool, dry place, which means that you should resist stashing it in the attic (too hot) or the basement (too damp). Consider placing your boxed gown and veil in a special trunk, kept in a room or closet that has consistent temperatures and little humidity.

OR . . . MAKE SOMETHING OF IT

A well-preserved wedding gown is an heirloom unto itself. But as keepsakes go, it isn't all that much fun because it can't be touched, admired, or displayed until another lucky bride in some distant future chooses to make it her own. There are alternatives to shuttering your special dress away in the dark; some are sentimental, some are practical, and at least one is philanthropic.

Frame it. Yes, it's opulent and expensive, but if you've got the financial resources and the space to display it, you can indeed have your dress framed and hung on a wall, just like any other work of art.

A Wedding Gown Is Forever

Transform it. More and more brides are choosing to have their wedding gowns taken apart and refashioned into something that's both useful and luxurious. You might consider having yours made into a keepsake quilt; a romantic drape atop a canopy bed; decorative linens for a bassinet; a communion dress; or a christening outfit.

Donate it. One bride of our acquaintance bequeathed her white satin gown to a convent, where nuns made it into altar cloths. Another shipped her dress off to Haiti, the most impoverished country in the world. There, the tradition of wearing a white wedding dress is so important that many women won't get married until they can afford to buy one or can collect enough white fabric to make one. Both of our generous friends say that by sharing their good fortune, they themselves felt blessed.

Little Things Mean a Lot

One of Kleinfeld's most extraordinary services is the creation of miniature dresses. If you've ever visited the salon, you've seen these tiny creations on display: they are eighteen-inch-tall exact replicas of individual bridal gowns, reproduced in exquisite detail by the same sewers and beaders who work on Kleinfeld's human-size gowns.

Kleinfeld started offering the trophy-height gowns after one too many brides bemoaned the fact that after one glorious day, their wedding ensembles were packed away and never seen again. The solution was a handmade replica, fitted on a miniature dress form, that could be displayed and admired day in and day out. The small-scale dresses, it turns out, were actually more difficult to make than their full-size sisters, and their average price runs from $600 to $1000.

Kleinfeld now sells ten or more miniature gowns per month, mostly to mothers or mothers-in-law as a gift to the bride. They're lovely keepsakes. The bride can always remember how beautiful she looked on her wedding day, without running the risk of ruining her actual dress.

LISA'S GOWN, PANDORA'S BOX

Lisa Reiskin came to New York from Maryland to seek her perfect wedding dress. She found it at Kleinfeld on a Sunday evening after a weekend of shopping with her parents and sister in Manhattan. "I wanted simple, elegant, sexy," says Lisa, "and this one was silky, strapless, and straight to the floor. Not like your typical wedding dress." Lisa's parents and their gracious host, Ronnie Rothstein, were "ecstatic" about her choice. "I was sure this was the dress," says Lisa. "It was so comfortable I could even lie down on a couch. So I said, forget the other dresses at the other stores in the city." The Reiskins put a deposit on the gown, returned to Maryland, and all was well.

Several months later, after Lisa had made another trip to Brooklyn for her first fitting, she and her fiancé, Brian Friedman, were lounging by their pool. "I still had stacks of bridal magazines," she says. "I was curious as to what kinds of dresses Brian liked, so I handed him some magazines and asked him to pick out his favorites." Brian, who had no idea what Lisa's wedding gown looked like, had trouble deciding which ones he liked best. "So I said, 'Pick out dresses that you wouldn't want me to wear,' " recalls Lisa. What happened next deserves a spot in the Bridal Nightmare Hall of Fame: Brian found an image of the exact gown that Lisa had chosen and said, "Definitely not this. I hate this one."

Lisa quietly freaked out. "I said to myself, 'I can't wear this. I can't walk down the aisle in a dress my future husband hates!' I was so miserable." She didn't let Brian know the awful significance of his choice, however. Instead, she went into the house and called her mother, who in turn called Kleinfeld.

Weeks later, Lisa and her family were back in Brooklyn. "It was supposed to be my second fitting, but Ronnie had heard the story," says Lisa. "He wouldn't let me be unhappy." With Ronnie's blessing, Lisa flipped through a new batch of designer gowns. "I fell in love with ten of them," she recalls, "but I knew right away that there was one particular dress that was going to be mine. It wasn't even a wedding gown—it was actually evening wear—but when I put it on we all knew. It had spaghetti straps decorated with tiny pearls, an empire waist with crystals at the bodice, a minitrain, and sheer overlays. It was simple, elegant, very sexy, form-fitting at the top—it made everything look good."

In March 2001, Lisa Reiskin donned her "new" gown, enhanced by a crystal-studded tiara and a layered veil, and became Lisa Friedman. "Brian was thrilled," she's happy to report. "He loved the dress, I loved the dress. So what could have been a disaster turned out to be an amazing experience."

EPILOGUE

Dear Bride:

We hope that *How to Buy Your Perfect Wedding Dress* has helped you in your wedding dress search. You may be thinking about the decisions you'll have to make regarding your dress, from choosing the fabric to selecting a style that won't shock your father or your mother-in-law. Our advice: Step back and relax. Remember to enjoy the day you select your dress, which can (and should) be as special and as enjoyable as the day you wear it.

At Kleinfeld, we pride ourselves on being with a bride from the moment she walks through our doors until the moment she walks down the aisle and says "I do." We believe that every bride should feel like a princess on her wedding day. So even if you can't personally visit us at Kleinfeld, you should choose a bridal salon that will treat you the way we've been treating our brides for over sixty years.

As a bride who has read this book, we encourage you to communicate all of your questions, ideas, joys and fears directly to us at our website (www.kleinfeldbridal.com), where we will personally answer your questions and endeavor to help you through this exciting—and sometimes overwhelming—process. We would sincerely love to hear from you.

With our warmest wishes for a happy marriage,

ACKNOWLEDGMENTS

When we were approached to write a book, we called Ken Browning, one of the leading entertainment and literary lawyers and entrepreneurs on the West Coast. He became our mentor, adviser, and "consigliere." It was our good fortune that Ken enjoyed a great relationship with Trish Todd, the editor-in-chief at Simon & Schuster, whom he called and said, "What about a great how-to book from the owners of Kleinfeld?" Trish said, "We've been thinking about this for years. Let's do it!"

We met Trish, a woman with integrity, great vision, and a keen sense of the market. Our book is her vision and ours. Without her very active involvement, this project would not have happened.

Working with Trish and with Simon & Schuster, one gets the benefit of working with many talented people. Karen Watts of Lark Productions and Todd Lyon (our cowriter), were the icing on our (wedding) cake. Todd is a gifted writer, interviewer, and researcher. A special thanks to Monica Rangne for her straightforward illustrations.

Both of us are always busy working with every bride and their families who come to Kleinfeld. We needed our personal eyes and ears to help us put the project together with Trish, Karen, and Todd . . . and that was our friend and Kleinfeld bride, Jennifer Parris, who is responsible for much of the creative work at Kleinfeld, and whose taste level and knowledge are trusted so much by us and our staff.

To our partners, who are among our closest friends and favorite relatives, we are grateful for your belief in Kleinfeld and in us.

A giant thank-you must go to the approximately 150 dedicated Kleinfeld employees who share our vision: *The day a bride purchases her wedding dress should be as enjoyable as the day she wears it.*

Each of our relationships with our bridal and evening-wear designers is very personal and meaningful to us. Our designers are very supportive of Kleinfeld and visit us from all over the country and the world for their trunk shows and other special events. We are glad they are a part of the Kleinfeld family.

We are also grateful to the media: the invaluable editors and publishers of the bridal and fashion magazines; the television reporters, producers, and anchors; and those informative bridal websites . . . you have looked kindly upon Kleinfeld throughout the years and have been wonderful to us.

And most important, to the twenty thousand or more

brides who have visited Kleinfeld each year from all over the country and the world, we sincerely thank you for making us such an important part of this very special day in your lives. For those who have yet to come, we hope that Kleinfeld can help turn your wishes into wedding dresses.

Acknowledgments

Notes

Notes

Notes

Notes

Notes

Notes

PHOTO CREDITS

ABOUT THE AUTHORS

RONALD ROTHSTEIN is the CEO of Kleinfeld, Inc. He graduated from the Wharton School at the University of Pennsylvania in 1964 and received his law degree from the University of Miami in 1968. In 1970 Ronald moved to New York and joined an investment banking firm, where he was associated for nearly two years. In 1972, Ronald, along with his father, brother, and two other partners, established a new investment banking firm. Ronald left the firm in 1976 and started a successful consumer products company named "Oh Dawn" that received national attention in *Forbes, The New York Times, Los Angeles Times,* and NBC's *Today* show. After selling "Oh Dawn" in 1986, Ronald and Arnold Perry formed Perry Rothstein partners, a boutique investment banking firm with offices in Los Angeles and New York. In 1999, Ronald Rothstein, along with Wayne Rogers, Mara Urshel, Clay Hamner, and Jim Clark, purchased Kleinfeld, the legendary bridal retailer in Brooklyn, New York. Ronald devotes all his time to managing the Kleinfeld business and strategizing its expansion.

MARA URSHEL was appointed president of Kleinfeld, Inc., in 1998 and was given the mandate to revitalize the sixty-year-old renowned bridal retailer. Having distinguished herself in the upper echelons of luxury retailing, Mara Urshel has enjoyed one of the most successful fashion retailing careers in America. From 1973 until 1992, Mara advanced at Saks Fifth Avenue, New York, to become senior vice president/general merchandise manager of women's sportswear, cosmetics, and fragrances. Mara also served as president of Geoffrey Beene Company and as chief merchandising consultant to Japan's Seibu Department Stores. As president of Kleinfeld, Inc., Mara Urshel brings years of experience and expertise in marketing and developing luxury merchandise. She directs Kleinfeld's day-to-day operations, including all merchandising selection, sales, marketing, advertising, and development of new business opportunities.